Celebrating the

100

Stories and memories
from 100 years of Crusaders

Urban Saints Support Centre, Kestin House
45 Crescent Road, Luton, Bedfordshire LU2 0AH
Telephone: 01582 589850 Fax: 01582 721702
Email: email@urbansaints.org
www.urbansaints.org
www.crusadersreunited.org.uk

Urban Saints is the operating name of The Crusaders' Union,
a registered charity in England and Wales (223798)
and Scotland (SCO39313)

ISBN No: 978-1-907636-41-7

Published by Verité CM Ltd for Urban Saints
Cover design, typesetting and production management
by Verité CM Ltd, Worthing, West Sussex UK
+44 (0) 1903 241975

Printed in England

My thanks for getting
the book off the ground...

Before you read on there are a few people that need to be thanked because without them you wouldn't have heard about the task that we had started. Much of the Christian Press ran a letter asking for editorial; Ali Hull inadvertently started the ball rolling with a seminar at Spring Harvest some years ago; Lesley Talbot gave secretarial support; David Morgan 'jollyed' the project along; Heather Williamson's work on the early submissions meant that editing was already underway when I picked it up. Thank you also to all the contributors without whom the book would not be!

Studland camp

Contents

Crusaders is 90! Alan Kerbey, Sir Cliff Richard, Heather Keep and Gilbert Kirby

About the Editor

My background is in Crusaders. My parents set up the class in Grimsby along with other leaders who had had a Crusader background and I started attending the class as it started. In its heyday our top numbers were over 90. We had the crazy games evenings, parties, days out, big birthday celebrations; we got involved in the Yorkshire Area for the swimming gala and I loved every moment of it. But the real highlights of my year were the holidays, first as a girl then as a Junior Leader and then Senior Leader and of course, Crusoe. In more recent years I have been involved in the New Year House Party at Westbrook, Smallwood and ReBuild Mexico. Working with young people, getting alongside them, seeing them have fun and finding more out about Jesus is just the best thing! But I am also extremely privileged to be a Trustee of Urban Saints which is quite a humbling experience and massive responsibility.

So how have I come to be involved in editing this book? Well, half of my degree is in publishing and my heart is in Crusaders! I have thoroughly enjoyed putting this book together for you. The amazing stories of people and their memories has been an absolute joy. The encouragement that is there on every single page of testimony, the impact that Crusaders has had on so many individuals, their experiences from across the world and in the fields of politics, popular music and sport – it is quite incredible! But I think what is more incredible to me, from a Crusader background but now involved in Urban Saints, is that what the organisation is doing now, the organisation was doing way back through

Albert Kestin, Herbert Bevington and all the other leaders involved in every decade. It just emphasises the song from Youth Praise that starts *'Yesterday, today, forever Jesus is the same. All may change but Jesus never, Glory to His Name...'*

I trust and pray that I have done justice to the task I took on, and that you will be encouraged again in the outworking of our Lord Jesus Christ through the stories that you read in the following pages, that memories will be rekindled and maybe friendships renewed.

Please enjoy and be inspired.

Ali Tompkins
Trustee / Editor

Sidmouth Girls Houseparty Summer 1959

The importance of remembering

They say that confession is good for the soul so here is my confession… I've never had a great memory. I often feel like the man who stood up to give a speech on growing old. He confidently began "There are three problems with growing old. The first problem with growing old is that you tend to forget things." Then he paused and said, "And you know, I can't for the life of me remember the other two points." Apologies for the bad joke but you get where I'm coming from.

My wife, on the other hand, seems to remember incredible amounts of detail. We might be holidaying in some small village in the middle of nowhere when Jo will remember that she's been there before and then start to describe some particular landmark in painstaking detail that soon enough we come across. But me – no! I write things on my hand so I won't forget. I set my phone alarm to remind myself to do something. Sometimes, and this is a little embarrassing, I leave messages for myself on my work voicemail. I don't have a great memory.

And yet remembering is really important, providing we're remembering the right stuff. God doesn't want us to dwell on our past failures, mistakes and sins. He has forgiven us from all that stuff. I love how someone once said how God drops our sin in to the deepest sea and puts up a sign that says 'No Fishing'. No, we don't dwell on sin because Christ has set us free from sin.

But there are important things to remember: Really important things that through remembering help us to keep on, keeping on in our walk of faith.

The Psalmist writes in Psalms 103 v2 ..."Praise the LORD, O my soul, and forget not all his benefits".

We remember God's promises.

We remember God's faithfulness.

We remember God's presence.

We remember God's kindness for breaking in to our lives time and time again, bringing healing and hope.

Jesus gave us the sacrament of communion – that we would remember Him – until He comes.

This is a book of memories. Great memories and stories from the history of Crusaders (now Urban Saints). A movement that for over one hundred years has been, and still is, passionate about helping young people live lives of faith, hope and love through Jesus Christ. This book captures story after story about how God has been at work across so many decades in this movement.

- We choose to remember yesterday because it encourages us to be thankful today.

- We choose to remember yesterday because it gives us faith for tomorrow.

- We choose to remember yesterday because by doing so we're reminded time and time again that God is for us. God is with us. God has plans for us. God ...is ...amazing.

If this doesn't want to make you join me in a hymn then nothing will...

Pardon for sin and a peace that endureth,
Thy own dear presence to cheer and to guide;
Strength for today and bright hope for tomorrow,
Blessings all mine, with ten thousand beside
"Great is Thy faithfulness!" "Great is Thy faithfulness!"
Morning by morning new mercies I see;
All I have needed Thy hand hath provided
"Great is Thy faithfulness," Lord, unto me

Amen!

Matt Summerfield
Chief Executive

Crusader Athletics April 1959

Westbrook, 1979

CHAPTER ONE

A Dedicated Leadership

'For you are a chosen people, a royal priesthood, a holy nation, a people belonging to God so that you may declare the praises of him who called you out of darkness into his wonderful light.'

1 Peter 2 v 9

I wonder what Albert Kestin's reaction would have been if he had known in 1900 that the legacy he started when he introduced those four boys to the Scriptures, would still be going strong and receiving the Lord's blessing over 100 years later. When we consider what was started and see how Crusaders came into being from that we can acknowledge that Albert Kestin was a truly inspirational man.

As far as the name 'Crusaders' came about, Mr Kestin happened to come across a picture of a medieval Crusader with both hands resting on a sword and the words underneath reading 'Be Strong'. The notion that Mr Kestin was involved in a crusade aiming to win the lives of boys for Christ seemed to explain what it was that he was doing. And so the name Crusaders was applied to the group that first started in Crouch End.

Albert Kestin was a dedicated, godly man who was concerned that boys were not hearing the Gospel message and that Sunday Schools were not meeting the need. However, he also realised his own need of needing someone to work with in leadership. That person was Herbert Bevington, who being like-minded recognised the work that

Mr Kestin had undertaken. He offered himself to work with the group of boys alongside Mr Kestin.

Albert Kestin returned to India as a missionary in September 1901 and left the leadership of The Crouch End Crusaders' Bible Class to Herbert Bevington, with the instruction that he was only to admit those boys not attending a Sunday School. Numbers increased steadily and news of this group spread around the London area. This in turn stirred up other Christian men to prayerfully seek the Lord's guidance and further groups were established.

By 1906 there were eleven independent groups with others planned. Mr Bevington had moved to the South Coast and other groups across the UK were starting. They were kept in touch by Mr Bevington circulating weekly 'Returns Sheets' which listed the attendance numbers of each group and included prayer requests as well as new of the possible formation of new groups. The Union did not come into existence until Albert Kestin had returned home from India in March 1906. The minutes of that meeting held in London outlined the responsibility of leaders for their classes, for teaching the Bible as the Word of God and retaining a keen evangelical message. It was agreed that the Union would work with all denominations and local churches.

Crusaders' has always been most effective with the outworking of relational youth work, whether that was in the 1920s or through to the early 2000s. The book of Titus chapter 2 and verses 6 to 8 describes our leaders pretty well.

But it is not just in the running of groups that leaders have given dedicated service to the organisation. Other voluntary work such as the stamp bureau raised the profile of Crusaders and raised funds for its running.

*   *   *

An Open House

Rev. David J Randall, Edinburgh Trinity Crusaders

One of the main things that stand out in my memory of Crusaders centres in the open-home maintained by our leader and his wife, Alastair and Helen McDonald. Their happy hospitality was a great blessing to many of us, even those who came from happy homes – just to have someone else ready to listen and befriend made an impact that has been a lasting inspiration and also an example.

I was a member of Edinburgh Trinity in the late 1950s and early 60s, and experience gained in Crusaders was a great preparation for my life's work as a minister. I have ministered in Macduff in the north-east of Scotland for 35 years and regard my early experience gained first as a boy and then as a leader in Crusaders as a highly formative influence on my life. Maybe people who throw open their homes and hearts have no idea of the lasting influence that may be made.

Other memories include weekend camps (when was lights-out supposed to be?) and games night (expending gallons of sweat!), but the central thing was the Sunday afternoon class meeting, which supplemented all that I received and learned in church. The teaching was good and fresh, but my most abiding memory is of this sense of acceptance and fellowship that was warm, welcoming and winsome.

Never underestimate the power of a good bookmark!

Eileen Fletcher, Edinburgh Trinity Crusaders

I was brought up in a Christian family, I knew a lot of Bible stories, I went to Sunday School and I also attended Edinburgh Trinity Girls Crusader class.

It was only when I was given a bookmark, dark blue with the Crusader badge on it and a text, that I began to see that the love of God was for *me*. The bookmark has long gone but the text has stayed with me over nearly 50 years and when I hear it read I want to shout "That's *my* verse!" The words are 'We love because he first loved us.' (NIV) 1 John 4 v19.

The leaders at Edinburgh Trinity, Miss Smith and Miss Anderson, could not have realised the long term effect. A simple gift to a child has brought a lifetime's gift of God's love.

*   *   *

Belonging... believing... begetting!

James Spanner (previously Handley), Ealing Broadway Crusaders

I was a member of Ealing Broadway Crusaders 1958-69, meeting first in the YMCA, and later the Methodist Church schoolrooms. One Sunday in 1967, leader John Baldock asked me if I'd like to go and hear Billy Graham that evening, to which I replied 'no thanks'. I don't know if he misheard me or was listening to another voice, but I later heard the horn of his Rover outside the house, and was too polite to decline a lift to Earls Court. That evening was the decisive turning point in my life as I went forward to commit myself to Jesus Christ.

Four years later, (now an engineering student and member of Rugby Crusaders), and having been to Cru Camp every year since 1962, I signed up for the summer venture run by Crusaders in Moss Side, Manchester. There I met Steph, daughter of Eastbourne Crusader leader Peter Pickett. One thing led to another, and we married in 1974.

In the early 80s, I trained for the C of E ministry, and am currently vicar of St Mark's Colney Heath, just outside St Albans. I tell my 'Crusader testimony' every time we have a 'Holy Spirit day' on our Alpha courses. We have 4 children, all themselves going on with the Lord and 3 (going on 5) grandchildren who are being brought up to know Jesus as their friend- a wonderful legacy that owes much to Crusaders and committed local leaders.

John Baldock died some years back, but his son Stephen (a phenomenal pianist who set CSSM choruses alight with his playing) went on to become High Master of St Paul's School, Barnes.

James Spanner and Steph (5th & 6th from left) with 4 children, three spouses, a fiancee and two grandchildren.

Nurtured and Guided

**Michael Flowers FRCS,
Sheffield Eccleshall/St Saviourgate, York**

I shall always be grateful to Crusaders. My elder brother had been converted at a summer camp at the age of twelve, and in 1945 I began to attend with him the Sheffield Ecclesall Class led by Godfrey Lake and Tony Benthall among others. I must have made their lives a misery with disruptive behaviour, but I could not fail to be impressed with their commitment to Jesus, the care with which they had obviously prepared their material, and their extraordinary patience and persistence with me and my errant friends.

When I was sent to boarding school in York in 1946 I attended the local class in the appropriately named St Saviourgate, slipping out of school unnoticed on Sunday afternoons with my Bible concealed inside my school cap. There I came under the care of Mr & Mrs Johnson who were such wonderfully enthusiastic and generous people.

He played a honky-tonk piano to such good effect that even self-conscious young teenagers were persuaded to sing those strange CSSM choruses with gusto. They regularly invited me to share their jam sandwich tea with them after the class. I was colossally impressed with their serenity and obvious joy in Christ.

It was they who encouraged me to go on a VPS cruise on the Norfolk Broads during the Easter holidays. I have no memory of the other five boys on the boat, but our "skipper" was a young man I remember as a Mr Butcher, an articulate and engaging person who made it his business that week to propel me into the Kingdom. I recall him asking me on day one if I was a Christian. I was taken aback, no one had asked me before, and I assumed that as I was brought up in a devoted Christian home, that would do. He replied that being born in a garage doesn't make one a car! And then he proceeded patiently to explain what a real Christian is. Over the rest of the holiday I was in turmoil because I could see that if I was to give my life over to Jesus things would have to change. I wasn't sure that I was ready for that. However, on the last evening, he pinned me down and I capitulated and prayed the prayer.

Easter 1949: that's when everything changed for me, and I'm so grateful to him, to the Johnsons, and the Crusader family that subsequently nurtured and guided me. Thank you God.

*   *   *

A Life Turned Upside Down

Barbara Fletcher
Wareham Crusaders/Ellesmere Crusaders

Has Crusaders made a difference in my life? Well – yes! In fact, through Crusaders my life has been turned upside down. But let me start way back in the 60s...

One of my school friends had told me about a new group that was starting in Wareham, the town where I lived. I went along out of curiosity – and loved it from the start. Finding out what was in the Bible seemed reasonable enough – after all I was a Christian; I'd been christened just like everyone I knew.

The leaders, Alan & Pamela Saunders, were great – always ready to open their home, fill the land rover with dogs and young people, and invest a huge amount of time, energy and, no doubt, prayer in us all.

I went off to an Easter house party in 1966 along with three of my friends. The evening meetings were a revelation to me, as I heard that God loved me but couldn't accept my sin. Life at that time was pretty hard; years of bullying had certainly taken their toll and I needed to know that love. As I thought through what I heard it all began to make sense. Yes, I was a sinner and deserved to be punished. Before I went home I'd heard that Jesus died on the cross to take my punishment and wanted to come into my life and make me a brand new person! Wow! *Really?* I want that too!

It was in floods of tears that Jesus came into my life there in Exmouth, and I *really did* feel like a brand new person. I'm forever grateful to God for such a vivid emotional experience, as the bullying didn't stop until I left grammar school. During those difficult times that experience of God's love and acceptance was there to comfort me.

Over the years, inevitably, there have been ups and downs in my life – times of doubt, struggles and questioning. But God has brought me through it all and life's certainly never boring!

I began helping with the Shirley group whilst teaching in Southampton. During that time God decided I needed someone to help sort out my confidence problem and gave me John. Together we were privileged to work on O.M.'s ship Logos, and whilst in Fiji our first child, Paul was born.

Eventually we ended up in Shropshire and soon the Ellesmere Crusader group began. Seventeen years later and we have been able to start a junior group in our village. We have launched an older group: God has been very good!

Crusaders has had, and *continues to have*, a huge effect on my life. Both Paul & our daughter Naomi grew up through Crusaders and are actively involved in outreach as adults. I will never stop thanking God that I met Jesus at an early age, and want to really encourage today's leaders that they're doing a brilliant job. Leading young people to Jesus is just the best thing in the world!

*   *   *

The Invitation of a Friend

Christine Wood

In 1932, shortly before my 11th birthday, my parents, brother and I moved from Essex to a brand new house in Surrey. At my new school I soon became friends with Wendy, who invited me to a Sunday afternoon Crusader class. 'It's nice. We sing choruses and listen to Bible stories,' she told me and, because I liked being with Wendy, I went with her.

Perhaps because I came from a non-Christian home and environment, the Assistant Crusader Leader impressed me deeply. She welcomed me warmly to her class and it seemed to me that the love of God shone through her as she spoke so sincerely of all that Jesus had done for us when He died on Calvary's cross. I drank in every word and before Christmas I surrendered my life to the Saviour who had died that my wrongdoings might all be forgiven.

By the time the Second World War broke out I had moved up into the Senior Class run by the Crusader Leader. The hall where Crusaders met was commandeered for war purposes and the class had to close. But Mrs Green, the leader, opened her home to several older girls on Sunday afternoons, of whom I was fortunate to be one. I sat under her teaching until she and her husband moved to Coombe Martin in Devon.

I married in the 1950s and by then another Crusader class flourished in Surbiton. The new leader asked me to help by teaching the juniors. This I did for about five years but eventually left to devote as much time as possible to writing children's books with a Christian theme (20 books in all). Upon publication of each book it gave me great pleasure to send a copy to Mrs Green – to whom I spiritually owed so much.

On a summer holiday in the early 1960s my husband I toured Devon. We spent a day in Coombe Martin, where we enjoyed a picnic on the beach with Mr and Mrs Green. I am so grateful we had that delightful reunion because Mrs Green died the following winter.

I vividly recall that while on the beach Mrs Green suddenly turned to me and said, "Had anyone told me when I started the Crusader class that one of my girls would become a Christian author I simply wouldn't have believed it."

I owe so much to Crusaders, where I was encouraged to accept Christ as my personal Saviour. The guidance and Christian teaching I received have shaped the whole course of my life.

* * *

A Devoted Leadership

Chris Porteous, East Dulwich Crusaders

I hated Sunday School and managed to escape from going from the age of eight until I was 11. Around 1948, I was invited to join the East Dulwich Crusader class which met in Townley Road East Dulwich and later moved to Dulwich Village. The attraction of Crusaders was in the quality of the leaders who were all laymen and business men but also very devoted Christians and very kind to me.

The Leader at the time was Jack Wales together with a Mr Taylor. I stayed at the Class until 1954.

However, after a year or so I was persuaded to go to Westbrook on the Isle of Wight returning a few more times. One year there was a fear of polio spreading among the campers; another year there was a thunderstorm in the night and torrents of rain which I slept through, but in the morning found half the tent had been evacuated because water was running in a stream through the half I was not sleeping in.

Going to Westbrook brought me in contact with boys and leaders from other classes especially Hayes where the leader was J.K. Anderson, a bridge engineer, who eventually became my next door neighbour in Beckenham. It was at Westbrook that I found the meaning of Christian fellowship especially through prayer and what the late Guy H King (my vicar and a vice president) called "sanctified common sense".

Having moved to Beckenham and become an Anglican reader in 1958, I became an assistant leader of the Beckenham class in 1959 and was blessed to have A.T. Bell, an insurance broker as the Leader. My time at Beckenham finished in 1963.

Crusaders taught me how to give talks, how to speak about faith and the importance of what was called personal work or pastoral ministry. I became the solicitor to the Commissioner of Police in London and head of the legal dept at New Scotland Yard from 1987 to 1995 and received a C.B.E in 1993.

I now live in retirement in Birchington Kent:

*   *   *

An Overwhelming Introduction

David Challen
Sutton Crusaders/Worcester Park Crusaders

December 1952 (when my school friend took me to Sutton)
continuously to July 1988 (when Philip and I moved from Worcester
Park to Chandlers Ford).

In 1952 my family moved to Worcester Park in Surrey. One Sunday morning a school friend called round to invite me to go that afternoon with him and other friends who went to Sutton Crusaders. Being a polite little boy (!), aged 13, I said yes, but immediately he had gone, I told my father "I don't want to go to any Bible class on a Sunday afternoon!" Dad said "you said you'd go, so you *will* go today. If you don't like it you don't have to go again".

We arrived. The gang introduced me to Randle Manwaring, standing outside the Sutton Cru Hall welcoming every boy with a handshake. 120 boys present! A hymn was announced. I enjoyed singing hymns, but was used at school assembly to the older boys mucking around, so was expecting the same. We started to sing. A huge volume of enthusiastic singing came from the Seniors at the back! I was shocked! It was the start of a completely new experience of warm welcome and friendship.

I went next Sunday and on arrival Randle said "hello *David!*" I was overwhelmed! He remembered my name! Even though we had not spoken since the initial greeting, as he was not in my section, and amongst 120 boys! What was it about all these men? They certainly had something special, everyone was so warm and friendly, and every boy seemed special.

In 1954 our gang became the core for new class Worcester Park, under Douglas Kahn's leadership. Douglas organised class weekend camps, and encouraged us to go on summer camps. That's probably where I made a personal commitment of my life to Jesus, but I cannot be sure.

Douglas was so effective in training us teenagers towards class leadership. My brother Philip (recently called home by the Lord) and I both became committed leaders at Worcester Park, and at summer camps, taking boys from the class with us, Philip to Westbrook, and me to Polzeath.

So my huge gratitude to Randle Manwaring, Alan Vaughan, "Mogul" Barnard, Brian Batten, Douglas Kahn, and many others, for living Jesus before us in the power of the Spirit, with enormous fun, complete integrity, and totally committed friendship. I really "caught" Jesus and the Christian faith from these men.

*   *   *

Wonderful Neighbours

Jane Locke, Dudley Crusaders

When I was born, the Abbiss family had just moved in next door. John was a leader at Dudley Crusader Class. He and his wife Vera were wonderful neighbours, and looked after me a lot, as my brother spent a lot of time in hospital when he was young.

Dudley Crusaders was a mixed class by the time the Abbiss's eldest daughter and I started going in 1973. We loved the Tuesday games nights, with table tennis, snooker, tuck shop and the darts board – which you had to dodge on your way to the toilet! The activities on Saturdays were great too – Netball competitions, ice skating, treasure hunts, trips in the summer and fab weekends away. The leaders were very committed, and put an awful lot of time and effort into our lives.

Crusader class was on a Sunday morning, 9.30 – 10.30. My memory is one of hearing that God's Word was very important to all the leaders and praying to God and reading the Bible was something they did every day. At first I was amazed that leaders, and some of the kids, would stand up and pray, and talk so naturally to God. I remember even at a young age of probably 9 or 10, feeling guilty when I prayed, and wanting God to forgive me, and to be right with Him. I was scared about what happens when we die.

In 1976 I went on my first Crusader Holiday, and in 1977 became a Christian on a Cru Holiday at Monkton

Coombe. My dorm leader asked us all to tell her at some point during the week, whether we were a Christian or not, which made me think, I should be.

I really wanted to go to church, and one of the Dudley leaders, Sam James, invited me to his church, where I started going in 1978. In 1981 I was baptised, which is when my Mum started going to church. It was some years later that she too became a Christian and was baptised, then my brother (who also came to Crusaders and went on Cru holidays). The Crusader PHAB holidays (1981 – 1985) made a lasting impression on me, and other friends from Dudley who came. It was wonderful to be able to serve and learn together.

In 1985 I finished University, and started helping at Dudley Crusaders, becoming a leader. In 1990 I met my husband (who's Mum had been a Mini-Cru leader in Letchworth!), and he became a Crusader leader. Dudley Crusaders had to close when our building became unsafe, but with the help of our Area Development Worker and a lot of prayer, Crestwood Park Crusaders began in 1993.

The Lord has influenced all of my life, and my family's, through Crusaders, and I thank God so much for those He has put in my path, and for the opportunity to serve Him and tell others about the saving love of Jesus.

*   *   *

Still Looking Unto Jesus

Karen Lloyd, Gerrards Cross Crusaders

My introduction to Crusaders was initially through a teaching colleague of my mum's when I was nearly 11. She introduced me to the girls group in Gerrards Cross run by the Scorers.

I became a Christian on a holiday camp over Easter when I was 11 and I had a great time. The young leaders and their enthusiasm made quite an impression on me. I still remember the talk on the last night about Peter getting out of the boat and putting his faith in Jesus. I decided that I wanted to give my life to Jesus then and there.

Every Sunday my dad would drop me off at 3pm. During the first part of the meeting we were all together for singing and group activities and then we would split into relevant age groups. We had great Christmas parties with an enormous Christmas tree which nearly touched the ceiling and had real candles which we took it in turns to light with a long lighter (before the days of health and safety restrictions). I faithfully went every Sunday and as the years went by was presented with the rewards for that from the bookmarks to the wonderful Bible which was a treasured possession. Not having Christian friends at school, Crusaders was my main support through my teenage years and a great help when I was faced with difficult choices.

When I was 17 I helped on my first camp in the kitchen. How can I forget the enormous grill pan, trying to keep up with toast for 65 people? The toast cooked faster and faster as the machine warmed up with me having to push the pan in and out at increasing speeds!

In my 6th form years we had a wonderful leader called Lyn Vernon who affected the whole of my life. When I was with her I felt that I was with a lady who really knew Jesus.

She obviously cared for us and I am sure prayed for our well being for that time and the future.

I have always felt that Jesus has had his hand on my life through some very difficult times. I feel very privileged that I had the opportunity to be introduced to Him at such a young age through Crusaders. I used to think that my testimony was boring, however I now realise that with this early faith I was saved from the effects of a harmful way of life and all the memories of this.

'Looking unto Jesus' is as relevant a motto today as it has ever been.

*   *   *

The Stabilising Influence

Charles E Perkins, Richmond Crusaders

It was about the year 1919 that I was introduced into the Junior Crusaders Bible Class in Richmond, Surrey. My father had lost his life in the last months of WW1. My brother, 5 years older, was fully occupied with his own college education and we then had little in common. Then my mother collapsed, turning to drink, and a housekeeper had to be appointed.

So at an important stage of my life I was like a small boat cast adrift on the ocean without captain or compass – except for the godly influence of a Crusader class. In those early days, naturally, I learned little of doctrine but I was taught to read the Scriptures and became familiar with hymns and choruses. Three Crusader camps at Felixstowe were also a great blessing. Thus a true faith in the Saviour developed, which has influenced and shaped my entire life, bringing incalculable benefits, guidance and safeguards.

I constantly thank God for the self sacrificing work of the leaders of that Crusader class all those years ago.

A Cheeky Invitation

Alison Wynne, Blackburn Crusaders

I joined Blackburn Crusaders in 1975. I had been a Christian for about 6 months when my sister and her friend were invited to Crusaders by Tom and Belinda Watson, two of the leaders. I asked if I could go too and they said 'yes', even though that meant they had to make two trips in their car to get us all there. We met in Keith and Yvonne Burton's house in Wilpshire. I remember the house being packed full of teenagers, all treating it like home. We split into a number of small groups for part of the time. There were groups all over the house – in the bedrooms, kitchen, landing – one group even met on the stairs. The overcrowded nature of these Sunday afternoon meetings didn't deter any of us; we kept coming and we kept bringing our friends – and if numbers were ever a problem none of the leaders ever showed it.

I couldn't find anyone to give me a lift after that first week, but having experienced the fellowship and the teaching, I wasn't about to stop going. So I walked. It took about an hour and a quarter (each way) and I managed to drag two of my friends with me – unfortunately they didn't stay. Looking back now it seems only a few short years, but it was a time that shaped me as a Christian. In those crucial first years in the faith, I received encouragement and instruction from Blackburn Crusaders. I am, and always will be, very grateful to the leaders for this – to Keith and Yvonne, Tom and Belinda, Dave and Julie, and Nigel and Kathy.

A few years ago I attended a ministry training course run by the North West Partnership of churches. It was a wonderful surprise to find my old Crusader leader, Julie, on the same course. I haven't kept in touch with anyone from Crusaders, and it was lovely to catch up. It brought back lots of lovely memories – of Crusader holidays; of bonfire night parties (one of the leaders had a field big enough for a bonfire and all of us and our families!); of singing Christmas carols to the neighbours around the area we met in; of all the great social times I could have with other Christians my own age.

I don't believe I would be the person I am today if I hadn't been cheeky enough to invite myself to that first meeting!

Faithful Women

Shirley Smith (Nee Smith) and Mary Hill (Nee Pickles)
Halifax Crusaders

My link with Girls Crusader Union (G.C.U.) began through Miss Dorothy Hall, who came to the Grammar School – then 'Crossley and Porter' in Halifax in 1946. She came to teach French and Scripture. She was a lively Christian lady who impressed me, and my best friend, Mary Pickles, so much that when she began a Scripture Union group there, we joined aged 11. She began a Crusader Class meeting on Sunday afternoons about a year later in 1946-47. We met in the Literary and Philosophical Rooms in Halifax Town Centre. The group grew as more joined us from school, and others brought friends. We numbered around 20-30 girls, enjoying Birthday celebrations with special speakers, one I remember was Major Batt. We occasionally joined up with groups in Bradford and Leeds for special events in the County including some boys groups.

Around 1950 we moved to a room above the Gas Showrooms in Halifax, and a new leader, Miss Betty Greatbanks who had come to C & P School to teach French and German, arrived. She began a small mid-week group in her house in Stanley Road, Kings Cross, where 6-8 of us met for Bible study and fellowship. She inspired us all to commitment to Christ and discipleship. She was later joined by Miss Doris Watkin who helped the main Sunday afternoon meeting for some time.

So my best friend and I were brought to faith, and God has proved so faithful down our 75 years! What a lot we owe to these faithful women who spared time and energy with this group of teenagers. We finally left the group to go on to college and university at eighteen.

The Long-Suffering Leadership

Andrew Pettigrew, West Kirby Crusaders

I joined West Kirby Crusaders in 1959/60 when I was aged 10 and I attended on a regular basis over the next few years, receiving my Crusader Bible on 9th July 1961 for regular attendance. Whilst I generally enjoyed the classes, the spiritual side of things never seemed to make much impact on me and I gradually drifted away, skipping classes to play football, unbeknown to my parents! The collection money they gave me was put to good use at the local sweet shop although I can't remember how I explained away my muddy shoes and dirty knees when I returned home.

Many of us had been sent by parents and didn't really want to be there. How those leaders put up with us mischievous youngsters I will never know and when I did infrequently attend, the tricks we got up to would have done credit to that old cartoon character Dennis the Menace. I'm sure that those leaders must have gone home on several occasions in a state of total despair after what seemed like wasted afternoons. At the time, I remember being bored stiff and wishing that the class would end, finding little, if anything, of interest. I attended some of the summer camps and whilst these were enjoyable, nothing was stirred in me spiritually. However, little did I know what was to come, thanks to those faithful leaders who were busy sowing the seed.

After several years 'playing' at being a Christian, I finally committed my life to the Lord on 13th January 1975 through the ministry of a lay reader in the Church of England. It was only then that I realised just how much I owed to those faithful leaders who had done so much for all us boys back in the early sixties and I began to remember some of the messages that I had heard over the years. I contacted my old leader Jack Todd, one of the most faithful men of God I have ever known and was delighted to learn that West Kirby were holding a 50th Anniversary Service in April of that year. Sadly, Jack died before I had the chance to thank him for taking such a personal interest in me.

If I could pass on any encouragement to today's leaders, it would simply be to keep on sowing the seed. You will rarely see immediate fruit from your ministry, but fruit there will be in due season.

*   *   *

A Desire to Continue the Work

Richard Lake

To a short-trousered 8 year old in the 1950's, who felt that Sunday School was not getting me to where I needed to be, my wise parents gave the opportunity of going to Crusaders as an alternative. There I met with a motley crew of other boys (it was a boys only organisation then) and an even more motley crew of leaders.

Regular, fun Sunday afternoon meetings in the YMCA building, with lively singing of choruses (Numbers 304 and 5 sung together *"In my heart there rings a melody"* and *"Jesus, Jesus, Jesus, sweetest name I know"*), deep discussions at "Keenites", camps (with foul latrine pits (!) and wide games), travelling to cricket matches and to the celebration in the Royal Albert Hall…

But it is the leaders who form the centre of my most enduring memory: Patrick Hinton, highly educated, with a plumy accent, Director of the family business of a chain of grocery stores which became a supermarket chain later on; Alwyn Harland, slightly "batty", who would look over his shoulder to maintain eye contact during conversations while driving his Ford Prefect; "Rip" Kirby, short, stout foundry man, blunt and down to earth in what he said, and others, whose names, faces and characteristics have not stayed so clearly.

What made these people so memorable was that, though they came from very widely differing backgrounds, and said things in very different ways, they were able to work together, and they all spoke and lived the Gospel. I cannot remember any one thing that any of them said, but what they said and what they did tied together, and was to do with the love of God shown in Jesus Christ for me!

To them all I owe a great debt of gratitude. They helped me to take the first faltering steps into deepening faith – a faith which continues to grow. And they gave me the wish to continue the work! So, here in North Wales, working with "our" youngsters, in whom it is good to see signs of deepening faith, too and the legacy continues.

A Sacrificial Life

Ray Bywaters, Watford Crusaders
Tribute written by Ian Wherry

Ray Bywaters was associated with Watford Crusades from 1927 until a few days before he died in 1984. Over that period, he devoted himself wholeheartedly to attracting boys to Crusader activities and subsequently leading many to the knowledge of Jesus as Lord and Saviour. Many would go on to prominent and professional careers, far and near.

Ray's many gifts and attractions were very varied, sometimes chaotic, sometimes not always going to plan, but always fun. The focus was the front room of his house, containing an endless source of interest for boys; stamps, cigarette cards, football programmes, railway books, glider and other model making and lots of "special events". Saturdays in summer saw him with his canoes on the nearby River Gade, all of 18 inches deep. Some were homemade, some were patched up, but a great time was had by all, and another recruiting angle.

Ray chose to devote the majority of his time and efforts to bringing the Good News of Jesus to boys, to the detriment of any potential career. After working with his father and in the stamp trade, following wartime service, he worked in the Crusader HQ book room at Ludgate Hill. Without any formal training or qualifications, he was a more effective home missionary than most others. His infectious cheerfulness, enthusiasm and patience have seldom been matched.

Every August would see him at Crusader Camp, with his orange tent and a selection of activities, a particular haven for the lonely, homesick or non-sporty boy. To travel to camp in his car as a passenger was a great honour and adventure!

He lived with his long suffering sister Mary, who often despaired of the unfinished jobs and the 'mess' in the front room, but always remained a stalwart, behind the scenes, supporter.

The point of all his activities was to interest and encourage boys to then come along to Crusader Class and camp and hear the Gospel message. His rich singing voice would ring out those familiar CSSM choruses. Follow up and home visiting was always diligently carried out.

By the time he died, it was already the twilight of his style of activities. Hundreds attended his funeral Celebration and his small memorial stone, of course, features a Crusader badge.

*   *   *

From Durham to 'Barney'

Steve Saxton, Barnard Castle Crusaders

My memory is of Barnard Castle Crusaders in 1970, soon after it was founded. Two or three of us, Durham University students, used to drive out on a Friday afternoon, help with the class, and stop over till Saturday for a Bible study, or social event.

The class met on Friday afternoon because the three schools in Barney (as the town was generally known) took pupils from a very wide geographical area, and it made sense to catch the boys while they were in town. But this did mean that the teacher who took the class was close to exhaustion, running on adrenaline, while the boys were demob-happy, and the atmosphere could be distinctly lively.

The three schools were a grammar, a secondary modern, and a public school, but there was little noticeable difference in the boys' style – they all mucked in and had a good time.

We met in a Methodist church hall with a rough wooden floor, which resounded to that Youth Praise classic *'When the road is rough and steep...* (clap clap)'. Other people clapped; Barney Crusaders stamped – both feet, the whole class, and made the building shiver!

The photo is of visiting speaker John Hartley, showing the acetylene lamp he used to use for his talks. As usual, the boys are taking the closest of interest – no such thing as personal space at Barney Crusaders. We took one Christian student out to meet the class (biggish lad, he was a prop forward), and four teenagers wrestled him to the floor and sat on him by way of welcome – all in fun!

I was only connected with the class for a year or so, but it's still a powerful memory.

* * *

Dedicated Christian Service

Terence Collings, Exeter Crusaders

During the late 1950s and early 1960s, I was a member of the Exeter Crusader Class as were many lads from the school which I attended, including some from my form. The Crusader leaders who stand out most in my memory were a solicitor, a medical practitioner and an estate agent. It was through their ministry that I asked the Lord Jesus to be my Saviour and Lord.

I am not sure whether, at that time, I fully appreciated how much time was taken up by their leadership commitments. If my memory serves correctly, at least two of them also devoted nearly a fortnight each year to being officers at a Crusader camp or house party. (I was able to attend a house party one year, on the Isle of Wight, and much enjoyed it.)

In my working life I never attained the eminence which they had reached although I have no regrets. But it has occurred to me in recent years that there may have been an element of sacrifice, additional to that of time, in their Christian service. In the social circles in which they would normally have moved, possibly not everybody was pleased that these men had a significant "leisure" activity in telling boys about Jesus. I am eternally grateful to them.

* * *

Faithful Spreading the Word

Arthur Oliver, Putney Crusaders

I was an only child but I was very fortunate in that my cousins, Harold, two years older, and Eric, two years younger than me, adopted me as their middle brother. Harold will always be special to me for it was he who introduced me to Crusaders. When I read Jack Watford's book, 'Yesterday and Today', I read it from cover to cover, fascinated by the number of people he mentioned whom I knew including Jack himself and Mr E.P. Olney who, as Leader of Putney Crusaders, led me to faith in the Lord Jesus.

I feel very humbled to learn how many Crusader classes many leaders have started, including several by Harold. We learn in 1 Corinthians 12 that God has given different gifts to different people to fit them for different jobs. I think that my gift must be 'Jack of all trades' for I seem able to turn my hand to all sorts of things, including lending a hand at various classes and at umpteen camps. I was also involved in the Sailing Camp on the Norfolk Broads. I often think, when I sing that Chorus 'The Lord hath need of me' how preposterous it seems that Almighty God actually needs poor little old forgetful me. But I am encouraged by the fact that the Lord Jesus found a use for that little four-legged donkey so long ago!

I am sure that Jack Watford was right when he wrote that the task before us now is far more difficult than it was 100 years ago. But 'With God all things are possible' Matt 19 v26. Peter Jeffrey told us so confidently that 'the best is yet to be', and I am sure that he is right. I keep rejoicing in that wonderful verse in Isaiah 53: 'He shall see the fruit of the travail of his soul and be satisfied'. The Lord Jesus will say, when it is all over that it was worth it: that he who, as we read in Hebrews 12, 'For the joy that was set before Him, endured the cross, despising the shame' despite all that things that we must have grieved Him by doing or failing to do, will rejoice in savings thousands of Crusaders down the years. And the best of it is that 'Nothing in all creation can ever separate us from His love' Romans 8.

*   *   *

An Inspiration and Passing on of a Legacy

Jocelyn Beale

I first heard about Crusaders in 2002 when I was 40! I had been invited to Barbara Atkins' house to join a prayer meeting and Barbara had just celebrated her 90th birthday!

After being introduced I sat down and Barbara asked me if I had ever heard of Crusaders. I said "No". She wasted no time in giving me a brief history, and of her involvement over the decades together with that of her late husband, Jack. Her love for the Lord and Crusaders was obvious, and she spoke about them each time I met her. I was curious to know more so she kindly got me an invitation to a Crusader Garden Tea Party held in 2003.

My own life has been rather full of its own trials and the journey has only been possible because of the unfailing 'Grace, love and guidance' of God and Jesus Christ. So Crusaders has made a big difference to me as a supporter because I know that children and young people in this country and the wider world are being given the all important 'Good News' i.e. God and Jesus Christ 'love you' and 'will never leave you or forsake you'.

Here's to the next 100 years, and beyond! And thank you so much for letting latecomers like me join in the fun!

*   *   *

Crusader Stamp Bureau

Keith and Jill Sharman

In the mid 1960's the late Harold & Olive Skinner of Seaford in Sussex re-established the Crusader Stamp Bureau, sending out stamp approval books to those Crusader contacts who had requested them, as a fund raising exercise for Crusaders.

About ten years later Harold and Olive felt it was time to pass the responsibility on to new and younger organisers, and after much prayer and thought Jill and I decided that this was an activity that we could undertake. We made the journey down from Cheshire by car and filled it with the current stock and returned to Warrington to set up the Bureau in a small and narrow room in our home. We continued to use the same procedures, making enhancements as we went along. The pricing structure for the approval books was on a sliding scale based on Stanley Gibbons catalogue prices, with 1p charged on entries of 5p; with 2p for entries of 8p etc – up to half price for entries of 50p and above. This procedure worked well giving cheap prices for the more common stamps.

As the Bureau became more established with us, many people started sending us packets and parcels of stamps. As both Jill & I were working and our boys at school, my parents agreed to undertake an initial sorting for us. They would sort into three categories – UK definitives (snipped with 1/8th border); UK Commemoratives (special issues e.g., Christmas) soaked off paper and put in bundles of 100 – all the same; and foreign by country. We visited Mum & Dad bi-monthly in Mundesley, Norfolk with bags of packets received and we would return home with bags of stamps in each of these categories. We made up parcels of definitives (in kg) and 1000's of commemoratives for subsequent sale to the wholesale trade. We mainly used two outlets, either Stamps for Evangelism, based in Derby which was convenient on our journeys to Norfolk, or Sandows in West London on visits to family in Surrey. The foreign stamps were put in our stocks for the approval books, with surplus items being sold by weight to the trade.

In the latter years we started to receive old stamp albums from friends and past Crusaders to enhance our fund raising efforts! There was no way that these stamps could be incorporated into our approval books, so we entered the business of selling complete albums to the wholesale market. After careful analysis of the possible outlets, we found Cavendish Philatelic Auctions in Derby where we received a sympathetic understanding – one of the senior staff had been a Covenanter Leader in the past.

After my father's death in 1986, my mother continued the sorting process for us for another 18 years. However at the turn of the century, it became apparent that the Bureau needed to move on. With no successor, despite advertising, we gradually allowed the Bureau to reduce its output and by Easter 2004 it ceased its operations. My mother was getting tired of her involvement, and she died in June 2005, aged 96.

As we look back over the period of the Bureau, we see many highlights in the contacts we made with all sorts of people – home and abroad. Occasionally we would receive cheques for hundreds of pounds, thus helping to raise a total of over £25,000 over our period of tenure of the Bureau. Although this activity was purely financial, it gave us great satisfaction in that we were supporting the work of Crusaders – so dear to our hearts and through which we both made our Christian commitment.

* * *

Photo taken from the Crusader Holidays brochure 1966

Stoke Fleming 1 1961

CHAPTER TWO

Building a Sure Foundation

'... in which you shine like stars in the universe, as you hold out the word of life'

Philippians 2 v15b – 16a

Crusader leaders made it their aim to instruct members of groups in the words of Scripture so that the boys were well equipped to face each day, as well as knowing Jesus as their personal Lord and Saviour. A support came from CSSM who had been persuaded to print and circulate a list of daily Bible readings suitable for children. This had come about because of a Sunday School teacher in Keswick who had explained how she had managed to get the girls in her charge to read a short passage of Scripture every day. She had written a list of suitable readings for the week, distributed them on a Sunday and then they discussed what they had read during the following week's Sunday School. The initial idea was first published in 1879 and the purchaser of the card automatically became a member of the 'Children's Scripture Union'. Crusader classes were encouraged to join the Scripture Union and read the appropriate passage of the Bible each day.

By 1930 it was decided that the passage published by Scripture Union was too long for younger members of classes to access. Jack Hoare of the Muswell Hill Class discussed the matter with CSSM who then kindly agreed to print a card suitable for Juniors.

As the years progressed, the Union introduced a 'Motto' for each year which took the form of a poster that could be put up somewhere prominently in the home as a reminder. Every year there was a picture and a Bible verse which was memorised and carried around in the everyday lives of Crusaders across the country and beyond.

Teaching the Scriptures remains an essential responsibility of anyone involved in Christian youth work, but for the organisation of Crusaders, this was and remains nothing new – it was there at the very beginning

*　　*　　*

Encouraged and Nurtured

Heather Keep
Assistant Director Crusaders/Whetstone Crusaders

A school friend took me along to Crusaders in Whetstone, North London when I was 12 years old. Little did I realise then the huge influence that the organisation would have on my life! The class then met in a fairly small café where each week some of us enjoyed sitting on the tables so that more could fit in the space! Soon after joining I became a Christian, but not actually through Crusaders.

I owe so much to the nurture, encouragement, Bible teaching and training I received from wonderful, caring leaders, like Barbara Atkins. She was such a prayerful, godly person and her love and friendship continued to be a great support right up until she died in her 90's. Training events, house parties, the Area Fellowship all played a huge part in helping me to grow in Jesus and encourage me into leadership in the group later, which I loved. I'll never forget the thrill of being a Junior Officer for the first time at a Ventnor Easter house party and seeing God working there. Friendships made then have continued throughout my life. What a blessing the Crusader family is!

It was such a privilege to be on the staff of the girls' work and later of the joint boys' and girls' work. I look back and thank God for men and women who were brilliant role models and for the many lovely people whom I worked with on the staff team and committees or came to know through their work in groups and holidays. There are memories of many changes down the years and learning much, especially about prayer, as we grappled with the ever-changing situation in our country and asked God to show us how to reach young people more effectively both here and overseas ... but always the same mission and message.

Most of all, there are many precious memories of God's amazing goodness and faithfulness. There were times of great highs and lows and 1976 will always stand out in my mind. The year began with Jack Watford receiving the MBE for his wonderful work in Crusaders as General Secretary and the girls' and boys' work merged, but in the summer there was great sadness when Peter Finnie, the Boys' Assistant Secretary, and Trevor Jones, Assistant Warden at Westbrook, drowned in an accident while trying out some new canoes in the Solent. A few months later, God blessed and encouraged us so much in the move from rented offices in London to a building of our own in St Albans, with all the money needed for it coming in just before the Thanksgiving Service.

Much of my work involved being in touch with leaders and nothing thrilled me more than to hear how young people were getting to know Christ and growing as disciples. This is what it is all about and it's wonderful to see how the work is continuing and developing in new ways – to God be the glory.

*   *   *

I thank my Lord God for Crusaders

David Wigner, Epsom Crusaders

I started at Epsom Crusaders Class in 1941. This was led by Christians who spoke my language and who obviously knew Jesus. I had asked Jesus into my heart before WWII started, and I had prayed each night with my parents and sisters in our air raid shelter during the Blitz in S.E. London. The WAAF took over our house so we moved to Epsom in May 1941.

I started to attend the Baptist Church regularly which was OK but Crusaders was terrific. The leaders included Barry Turner, Dr Aitken in Army uniform and Peter Mills (later MP). Junior Leaders included Arthur Mortimer who invited me to tea having done Home Guard manoeuvres on a Sunday morning, and David Dent, who played the pedal harmonium. We met in the primary school in Ladbroke Road, adjoining Rosebery Park. I remember being expelled for 2 –3 weeks for burning a dead bird in the park. Service men returned for various reasons including Dennis King who came back badly wounded from the RAF and played the piano. Others returned from their duties telling of experiences that they had: One returned from North Africa and told how he had had communion with another using oil drum as table, ration biscuit as bread and an army mug of water. This meant a *great deal* to me and has been probably one of less than half a dozen most important events in my life. *Marvellous!*

I found the emphasis on the Christian's armour very helpful, and I did ask the Sprit of the Living God to fall afresh on me – again and again: presumably He did in spite of my continuous failures at Epsom Grammar. Thank God for Crusaders.

We moved to N13 in July 1946 so I joined the Southgate Class which met in the Village Hall, led by Ernest Dyer and Henry Lawrence. This was the first class to camp at Westbrook with many of us sleeping on the concrete floor of an old hall. I found that when I attended the leaders and seniors prayer meeting after class I had a better week at Highgate School where I let down my Lord quite often. The encouragement of Harold Edmonds was of great significance – to teach Juniors.

The family moved to Bexhill-on-Sea in 1955 and I joined the Class led by Dr Leslie Scott, Roger Flowers [in his wheel chair] and Geoff Martin which met in Victoria Hall. Eventually I was a leader and I learnt so much about our Lord and Saviour Jesus by preparing talks for each Sunday. I left prior to 1970 because of the closure of the railway line to London, where I had to find lodging.

Later in life I was able to be Tent Officer at Studland and Westbrook, Canoeing on the Hamble, and at Castleton, Isle of Man. During the 1990s I was able to help at the class at the Royal Alexander and Albert School, Reigate for a few years.

Preparation for the Future

Hugh Amis, Guildford Boys/Gidea Park Crusaders

If asked what has been the greatest influence in my life, I could answer Crusaders.

My introduction to Crusaders was at a recruiting evening run by Guildford Boys group during the war years. Whilst I had been taken regularly to church as a child, this had meant nothing to me, and it was only in Crusaders that I first began to understand the Bible.

Guildford was a boisterous group and great fun. I particularly remember outings, camps and parties during those war years, but also being introduced to the practice of daily Bible reading and a 'quiet time' as we used to call it. I also recall the hearty singing of CSSM choruses, many of which I still remember in my seventies.

After the war we moved to Essex and in my mid teens I joined Gidea Park Crusaders. This was a much smaller group than Guildford, and rather better behaved! On Sunday afternoons we would have a formal meeting with choruses, hymns, bible reading, prayer and a talk, very often by a visiting speaker. Here we, as boys, were given the opportunity to lead the meeting, first by just announcing the choruses and then later by chairing. When older I realised that this had given me a foundation for public speaking.

We had Bible studies during the weekend also the occasional 'squash' on a Saturday, when we would meet in the home of a leader and listen to an evangelistic talk. All the activities were steps towards my becoming a Christian and after leaving school I became an assistant leader at Gidea Park.

Through an advertisement in the Crusader magazine, I went on holiday to the evangelistic conference centre Hildenborough Hall. This in turn was a step towards my joining an evangelical church where I met my wife. After some eleven years of marriage and three children we moved from Gidea Park to the Essex coast at Thorpe Bay, where both my wife and I were Crusader leaders for many years. We also had a fourth child there!

Crusaders has been great for our family life, as our children were with us whilst we were active leading a group. As Crusaders themselves they were able to join us for weekly meetings, various outings, Crusader Norfolk Broads cruises and squashes in our house, where we had as many as 60 teenagers listening to evangelistic speakers. Our three daughters all married crusaders and are active in Christian service. One is currently a leader of Hove group.

I found being a Crusader a great talking point in my business years, often leading to deeper conversation regarding the gospel. Crusaders has also given me a wider view of the church and an ecumenical outlook. My Christian faith was born in Crusaders, and I have a Christian wife, Christian children and Christian grandchildren. I am so grateful for being taken to that recruiting evening some 65 years ago.

*   *   *

Life-Changing Choruses

Valerie Luff, Westcliff on Sea Crusaders

Just before the Second World War I was persuaded by a school friend to join the local Crusader Class at Westcliff-on-Sea. Then in 1940 our school was evacuated, and there were no more classes. I rather drifted from my Christian roots.

About a year after the war, well into my General Nursing training, I was in the Nurses Home sitting room one Sunday evening when some of the girls started singing choruses round the piano, ones I had learned at Crusaders, so I joined them. When they were about to start their Bible Study I was walking out, but was invited to stay by one of my contemporaries, and what I heard convinced me that this lot had something I hadn't got, and I wanted it. Within a few weeks one of the leaders brought me to the point where I put my trust in Christ and asked Him into my life.

What a moment! Apparently some of my colleagues started, saying, "What's happened to Luffy? She's different." It certainly was a complete change of direction, leading after a few years to working on the mission field in Pakistan and India for about thirty years.

Since retirement I have helped at a few Crusader holidays in the 1990's, immensely enjoyable, and the group I served with still send me a postcard from the holiday every year. I think you can say it all started with Crusaders.

*   *   *

A Sown Seed

Sarah Labridis, nee Everett – West Kirby Class

I lived in Cheshire and attended Crusaders every Sunday with my sisters.

I remember one particular Sunday when our leader Doraine Wilkinson was talking about Jesus and I could see how much she loved Him and how her face shone. She asked us to invite Jesus into our heart and I remember feeling that I really wanted to do that but I didn't really understand how. I was about 10 years old at that time.

We moved away to the south of England and I attended a local church. I then moved to Greece and married there and had my children. I lived through an extremely difficult time in Greece, and knew that things were not as they should be and that something was missing.

In desperation, I prayed that if there was a God, I wanted Him to help me as I couldn't go on. I was immediately filled with an immense peace and although I didn't have any answers to my numerous problems I knew that I was not alone and that somehow things would work out.

I remembered back to that day at Crusaders 23 years previously and I realised that I had in fact asked Jesus into my heart all these years later and I had found the piece of the puzzle that I had spent years looking for. I was so thrilled and wanted to let my Crusader leader know that the seed that she had planted on that particular day had finally born fruit. Needless to say she was just as excited as I was and we have since stayed in touch. I have now been following Jesus and He is making up for the years that were lost. Although the problems didn't disappear, He gave me the strength to deal with them and go from victory to victory in my life changing the lives of those around me. Our lives only become meaningful when we know Jesus and His unconditional love and we live for God's glory.

A New Venture

George Court, Bowes Park Crusaders

I had the good fortune to be born into a Christian family – the youngest of four.

I believe my parents came from different religious backgrounds, one from Anglican, the other from Non-Conformist – I forget which way round – so I was brought up in an ecumenical atmosphere as well as being naturally inclined that way.

Our parish church was 'high' (incense etc) and, although I did not realise it until later, so was the 'tin' (corrugated iron) daughter church we mostly attended. Although I was not much of a singer, I was in the choir and later cross-bearer and server. In my teens I came to think I had 'grown out' of Sunday school and took to taking long Sunday afternoon walks in the belief that God could be found just as well in the countryside as in church.

At the age of 18 I was studying engineering evening classes at the Northampton Polytechnic in Islington when a fellow student Henry John Bond, a member of the large Wallington Crusader Class invited me to join him at a campaign meeting conducted by Captain Reginald Wallis at Finchley Class. There I learnt the difference between 'belief' and 'trust' and, overcoming my embarrassment, went forward with younger boys when invited to witness my decision to trust in the Lord. We used the prayer:

> *"Into my heart, into my heart, come into my heart,*
> *Lord Jesus, come in today, come in to stay.*
> *Come into my heart, Lord Jesus."*

We were each given a booklet by Captain Wallis entitled *'The New Venture'*.

I remember when travelling home from that meeting in the trolley-bus thinking that this might only be an emotional response which would disappear overnight and that I would forget about it in the morning. Thank the Lord that it did not do so and my sister months later was able to remark on how my life had been changed.

The Sunday after that Friday meeting, I went to the small local Bowes Park Crusader class which was in the hall of a local private school. This was led by Jimmy Jeffrey who had been at Southgate County School with my brother Walter, who was my senior by 12 years (and my childhood hero).

Shortly afterwards the class was led by Dr A.P.L. Blakely (Philip) from Southgate. His assistant was Alan Cobden – the owner of a fast ALVIS sports car. On one occasion he took us for a run on the newly opened North Circular Road where he achieved the amazing speed of 70m.p.h. which my father thought was too fast for safety (he was probably right!)

As a class we supported a missionary Rev Leslie Harwood who, with his wife, was working in Bolivia. I acted as class secretary for the Eastern Bolivian Fellowship run by Mr J.F.Higgs of Chiswick Class.

*   *   *

A Lasting Influence

Margaret Brierly

I became involved with Crusaders in 1944 at the age of 12, when the boys met separately, so I was in G.C.U. (Girls Crusader Union). Coming from a non-churchgoing family, and never having been to Sunday School, I was taken (quite unwillingly!) to the class through the parents of a girl in the class who I knew only slightly. I was very shy and nervous.

I was converted through Rev 3 v20, 'Behold I stand at the door and knock; if anyone hears my voice and opens the door I will come in and eat with him and he with me' and this altered the whole course of my life. I trained for full-time parish ministry, married an Ordinand and worked alongside him (N.S.M.) ultimately becoming a Deaconess.

I could write a book about the influence of Crusaders on my life. Yes, Bible teaching, yes 'camps' (not canvas ones but house parties at schools), yes friendships, yes joint Crusader Fellowship meetings with the boys.

*   *   *

A Grateful Influence

Rev R Michael Frost, Sutton Crusaders

I was born and brought up in Sutton (Surrey) and went to the Crusader class on Sunday afternoons in a hut close to the station. Wilfred Brown (solicitor) who lived in Wallington was the leader – a charming and godly man. Others on the staff were A.J. Barnard (Mogul), Hugh Ratcliffe (a gentle giant) and Lionel Hitchin. My cousins went to the Class at neighbouring Cheam.

In between leaving school and joining the Army I was employed in the Bank of England. I was called up in 1942 joining the Army in Canterbury. Ken Sweeting (a local chemist) led the class and I enjoyed the warm hospitality of him and his wife in their home. In the course of time I was posted to Guildford. The Class there was something special if only because of its amazing leader Mr Pimm (or 'Guv' as all the lads called him). He loved fooling about with us and yet, when he gave a Bible talk, we hung on every word as though life depended on it. I recall "Sammy" Senior who was, in his own way, quite a character too.

I recall as well that there was an Annual Meeting at Central Hall Westminster – always a great occasion. In addition we had an annual outing. The year I remember was when we went to Crewe railway works; on the return journey our special train was pushed into a siding so that we had a grandstand view of "The Flying Scotsman" passing through at top speed. The General Secretary was A.J. Vereker who lived in the Isle of Wight, and published an excellent monthly magazine. Those were the days!

As soon as the war ended I was accepted for the Baptist Ministry, trained at Spurgeon's College and ordained in 1949 – 62 years ago!

I owe a lot to Crusaders which played an important part in my Spiritual development in those days. It was uniquely fitted for the needs of private school boys and I shall always be grateful for its influence.

*   *   *

Crus' was my life

Muriel LeRoy

From age 7? to 75 years, 'Crus' was my life, blessing and joy, as well as home and family (Father was President after the Second World War); starting in Gipsy Hill in 1921 and finishing in Bristol in 1989. I followed father as Crus President later in life.

*   *   *

The Rock to Stand Firm On

John M Barnes, Ilford Crusaders

I joined Crusaders in 1931 at the age of 13. I felt that Crusaders offered more than the local Sunday school, although the Superintendent was a very godly man.

The Ilford Class commenced with the singing of choruses, followed by Bible reading and Bible searching; the leader read a passage of Scripture and we boys were asked to ascertain from which part of the Bible it came from – Old or New Testament, a letter to a church, one of the Psalms, etc – we were given clues along the way. Before a Bible reading we were always invited to offer a short prayer "Open our eyes that we may behold wondrous things out of Thy Law". There were several competitions running for which points were awarded (and a prize given). A short talk concluded the session, presented by one of the leaders.

There were Summer Camps on offer – one of the earlier ones was in Studland Bay and Westbrook on the Isle of Wight. The annual Sports Meeting at Motspur Park was a must, and there was friendly rivalry amongst the Classes; some of us envied the 'big' classes in those days, Wallington (Surrey) 200, and Finchley (N. London) well over 100. [Ilford Class never exceeded 59 boys!]

In addition to Union Sunday Meetings when there was a combined meeting of parents and friends and boys and girls from the local boys and girls Crusader Classes, Annual General Meetings held at the London Central Methodist Hall were always very encouraging to those who attended – some people travelled long distances.

For older Crusaders many of us enjoyed the 'Squashes' which, for our class, met at the home of the Snaresbrook Leader (the late Harold Ling) when almost a hundred boys and girls engaged in social and spiritual activities.

Boys who aspired to Class leadership had to be prepared to meet the General Committee of the Crusaders Union and face challenging questions as to their ability and suitability to take on this important and significant role.

My abiding memories of Crusaders was that it strongly encouraged regular Bible reading, with the prayerful hope that it would lead to full commitment of one's life to the Lord Jesus Christ. It certainly worked and prepared me for the Armed Forces, which came all too soon in 1939. It was said that Service life would either make or break you if you were a Christian before you enlisted. After demobilisation and before (and after) early retirement I was privileged to become heavily involved in several Christian Unions, finally serving as Hon. Secretary of the Federation of London Christian Unions.

*   *   *

A Showbiz Life Grounded In Jesus

Sir Cliff Richard, Finchley Crusaders

What a massive amount I owe to my days at the Finchley Crusader Class way back in the late sixties and early seventies. So many "firsts" – surely the first and only time that a Crusader badge featured prominently on a "Top of the Pops" performance, seldom has a sleek black Cadillac suffered the indignities of having its electric windows squirted up and down a thousand times by a bunch of lads en route to an Easter cruise on the Norfolk Broads. And there was podex at Polzeath, eleven up on an E-type Jag swerving around the camping site and sailing at Herm – things I'd never done before and have never done since – I might add!

They were extraordinary, heady days for me and wonderful restorative therapy from the wild and glitzy world of show business and early rock'n roll that would surely have devoured me if I'd let it. Believe me, there's nothing like a few teenage boys to heave you back to the real world and to shatter any delusions of self-importance that agents, PR moguls and fellow celebrities would have you believe!

My Crusader involvement not only kept my feet on the ground but was instrumental in giving me a grounding in the business of the Christian faith. I joined Crusaders to sit in the back row of the Sunday afternoon class specifically to listen to leaders give their twenty minutes talks. I lapped it up. It was what I needed; what I wanted. Occasionally I'd take my guitar along and lead some CSSM choruses – but most of the time I just listened.

When I moved away and left Finchley Crusaders a few years later I'd become an assistant leader, and this time at the front of the class I'd hesitantly give my first talks – sharing with kids what I'd learned from other leaders, what I'd learned from regular Bible reading and most of all, what I'd learned about the reality of Jesus who I'd got to know for myself and who has been real to me throughout my career and remains so to this present day.

*　　　*　　　*

A New Master

Peter Barker, Strawberry Hill Crusaders

Strawberry Hill Crusaders, South-West London, was about 100-strong in the pre-war years; the leader was Malcolm Wiles, an accountant, who led with tremendous conviction and with enviable rapport with 7s to 14s. He had an ancient car with an imitation-leather hood and when we went to play 'podex' or wide games in Bushy Park any young Crusaders who didn't have bicycles piled in; we called it "The Chariot".

The reliable and very competent pianist was Malcolm's brother Austin, who worked in a bank; through him we came to know and love the range of some 400 CSSM choruses. They were brief, some only four lines, some eight or more, all packed with theology expressed in accessible, popular language. Before the talk for the day "chorus time" was the climax of our afternoon – we sat and waved frantically as we tried to attract Malcolm's attention to approve each boy's individual choice for the next item. I never had my own chorus book, but those words have remained with me for a lifetime:

Yesterday, today, forever, Jesus is the same
All may change, but Jesus never, Glory to his name!

The Lord hath need of me, his soldier I will be
He gave himself my life to win and so I mean to follow him
And serve him faithfully.
So although the road be hard and long
I'll follow on, he makes me strong
And then one day his face I'll see
And oh! the joy when he says to me
"Well done, my brave Crusader".

Out there amongst the hills, my Saviour died.
Pierced by those cruel nails, was crucified.
Lord Jesus, thou hast done all this for me:
Henceforward I would live only for thee.

I once attended the summer camp at Sidestrand, near Cromer, on the Norfolk coast, I was never aware of the call of the Lord Jesus. Ten more years passed without my hearing the call. But in the army I first began daily Bible reading, after a year I realised that I wasn't yet a Christian; then in Somaliland one Sunday night I prayed, "Lord, if you're there, I need you" and the result was a that a new Master found me. There followed 30 years' service in Ghana, ordination in the Presbyterian church, and running a new publishing house, Asempa Publishers.

I know those later years were the outcome of three years attending Crusaders at an early age, for which I thank you, Lord!

*   *   *

Preparation for Life in Politics

Stephen Timms MP, Farnborough Crusaders

In 1968, I was 13. My younger brother, Roger, had joined my school, Farnborough Grammar. The Leader of Farnborough Crusaders, Tony Waterfall, came to tell us about the group. We all listened politely. To my consternation, Roger went along the following Sunday. He enjoyed it – and I decided I had better go too.

It proved a very formative decision for us both. We heard the Christian message explained clearly week after week. The leaders of the group committed enormous effort to it. Tony Waterfall and another leader – Tony Cottingham

– were scientific civil servants at nearby Royal Aircraft Establishment. Andrew Bradley was a young maths teacher at our school.

And we started going on Crusader camps. Farnborough Crusaders had its own annual Whitsun camp in a field on a muddy shore near Lymington. There, a year or so later, I decided that I wanted to base my life on this Christian message. We went to Westbrook, Isle of Wight. I went on a wonderful "Six Glens Trek" in Scotland, led by David Greenwood of Seaford Crusaders, a manager with Barclays, and another Scottish trek the following year. The beauty was breathtaking, the experience awesome, and the opportunity to think more about this new way of life I had entered very important too.

Our parents – not Christians – could see that what we were doing at Crusaders was worthwhile. So our Dad in particular ferried us backwards and forwards so we could take part.

About 1973, I wrote a letter of complaint to the Crusaders Union which was subsequently published in their magazine. The annual report had explained that Crusaders aimed "to bring into our ranks the Grammar School boys of tomorrow". That struck me as very unfair. What about my friends who did not make it to the Grammar School? Why should they miss out? (I don't seem to have been troubled by the implied exclusion of girls, though a girls' group did start up in Farnborough while I was there.)

We attended big rallies in London, and early concerts of "Musical Gospel Outreach". We started to read "Buzz" magazine, "The Cross and the Switchblade", "Run Baby Run" and Michael Green's brilliant polemical IVP books.

Because of Crusaders, I joined the Christian Union when I started at Cambridge University; through that I took part in a mission in Newham, east London in summer 1976;

as a result of that I went to live in Newham after I graduated. And that led to me becoming Leader of Newham Council from 1990 to 1994, one of the Newham MPs since 1994 and a Minister in the Labour Governments of Tony Blair and Gordon Brown from 1998 to 2010.

And the simple, but profound, convictions I formed at Crusaders have been the foundation for all I have done.

*　　*　　*

A Privilege to Serve

Rev Steve Walton

Wakefield Crusaders

 *UCCF travelling secretary 1980-83;*
Ordained in the Church of England 1983;
Curate, Bebington Parish Church 1983-86;
Vocation and Ministry Adviser, Church
Pastoral Aid Society, 1986-92;
Tutor in New Testament, St John's College,
Nottingham 1995-99;
Senior Lecturer in Greek and New Testament Studies, London School of Theology (formerly London Bible College) 1999 – present (Lecturer and Senior Lecturer)

I am enormously grateful for the help, kindness, care, support and opportunities for Christian service that Crusaders gave to me at very formative and important stages of my life.

My two years in Wakefield Crusaders was at a critical stage of life, during my A levels, and all kinds of things have flowed from the four leaders' patient, gracious and wise help in 1971-73. I had grown up in a rather sleepy village Anglican Church, and from the leaders, Elizabeth Ewan, Meuryn Walker, John Bullimore and Chris Kinch, I learned what an active, engaged personal walk with God can look like, the importance of Scripture to living as a Christian, and how to read Scripture in a thoughtful and relevant way. I am truly grateful to them for the Friday and Sunday evenings we spent together, and for the imaginative and thoughtful reading of the Bible we did together. They gave me a hunger to learn more and to serve God better, and much of what I am and do today has its roots in my two years in Wakefield Crusaders.

Looking back, I am also quite amazed that they stuck with me at the time, for I was frequently rude, arrogant and highly critical. I am quite sure I must have been very hard work indeed as a member of the group, and I am astonished at their patience, which I am sure must have been stretched at times to breaking point.

At University in Birmingham I became involved in helping at Moseley Crusaders (1973 – 1976) and greatly valued the chance to help Brian, Val and Kate in teaching and helping younger people meet Christ and grow. During my summer vacations at Birmingham I also served on Crusader holidays at Westbrook as a tent leader, and grew enormously through living alongside and communicating the gospel to young people. Key people on the summer holidays, notably Martin Horder and Bob Jackson, taught me how to do this well.

I'm enormously grateful for all these people's input in setting me on the path that led to Anglican ordination and, for the last sixteen years, teaching in theological colleges, having the privilege and fun of training people to lead and teach others.

I hope in due course people whom I have had the privilege of working with, in youth work or as my students, will want to thank God for me as much as I thank God for you. May the Lord bless you richly for your generosity of spirit, your giving of your time, and your sharing of your lives and homes.

Jesus became the centre of life

Trevor Roff

"What a strange place!" I thought as I entered the converted classroom that each Sunday housed the local Crusader group. In fact, the room had been twice converted; firstly from a residential conservatory of a substantial house in the middle of suburban Surrey into a rather dilapidated and old-fashioned classroom, then secondly into a meeting room for the weekly Crusader class. That explained why my first sight of the room was of dark, old Victorian style desks stacked up at the back of the room to make way for the Crusader meeting. What were my impressions of that first visit? A distinguished middle-aged man calling out numbers to indicate which of the CSSM choruses we were to sing next; a much younger man thumping out the tunes with great gusto but questionable harmonies; an old man standing up to tell us which team was in the lead for attendance and other achievements, showing the results with piles of nuts which the two teams' mascots were avidly stockpiling. It was bewildering, and amusingly quaint, but as my mother insisted I attended the class every week as a sort of penance for my escaping Sunday school by becoming a milkman's delivery boy, I supposed I had better make the most of it.

Within a few weeks I had found my feet, enjoyed the enthusiastic singing, wanted my team to win the quizzes and competitions and even began to wonder what the leaders were on about in their weekly talks. Over the next few years, Friday socials with table tennis, Sunday teas with the class leader, late night hikes chasing imaginary wild animals, and even hunting the "crack of dawn" in the Surrey countryside at 4am became my regular and much-loved itinerary.

And then there were the Crusader holidays! Every January I learned to look out for the latest brochure of exotic vacations offered and would spend hours poring over the various destinations on offer. Bembridge, See London, Westbrook, Wales, Scotland, hiking in France, even building a pipeline for a Christian orphanage in the Atlas Mountains of Morocco; these were and remain some of my life's most treasured memories. And Westbrook will always be a special place for me as it was there in 1963 that I at last let Jesus into my life.

That Crusader class eventually had to close as the privately run school it was held in changed hands. We then met in various homes (including that of a mature teenager who later went on to run Greenbelt and is now a well-known Anglican bishop.) But although we all went our separate ways I subsequently met up with or have written to a number of the leaders or fellow members and was always enriched by their renewed friendship and encouragement. Like many of my peers, I will always remember fondly those years when I got so much fun out of growing as a young Christian and learning to make Jesus the centre of my life. All because of Crusaders!

Studland 4 1961

Westbrook

CHAPTER THREE

Sundays at 3pm

'Therefore go and make disciples of all nations, baptising them in the name of the Father and of the Son and of the Holy Spirit, and teaching them to obey everything I have commanded you.'

Matthew 28 v 19-20

The traditional Crusader meeting started at 3pm on a Sunday afternoon and in most cases ran for the duration of term time rather than throughout the school holidays. Having said that many groups did run through the holidays and offered something different to the usual Sunday afternoon meetings.

Leaders would be at the entrance of the meeting place to greet each boy with a friendly smile and a warm handshake. There would be notices to read.

Sunday meetings across the land had a very similar format to them. In the early days, there was great excitement within classes as to which classes had the largest numbers attending, as the Returns Sheet was read out. The aim of each class was to grow and climb higher and higher up the list.

Promptly at 3 o'clock the leader would sit down behind a desk with rows of boys facing him. For the following hour or thereabouts, there would be hymns, choruses, maybe a 'sword drill', quiz, talk, Scripture reading and prayer. The boys would be encouraged to choose choruses that they enjoyed and they would sing along to with enthusiasm.

As the years went on, the Union awarded boys for their committed attendance each week. At 10 weeks there would be a Crusader badge presented, at 25 weeks a New Testament, but at 50 weeks it was the coveted embossed Bible that was presented. In the group I attended each presentation was celebrated by that well known chorus from 'Sing to God' *The Lord Hath Need of Me*, which has been cited in many of the stories.

But it wasn't just the Sunday afternoons. There was a lot going on around the Classes during the week as well. Many groups had mid week Bible studies, or activities during the weekends. There were inter-group events and competitions that supported the work of Groups.

Prior to World War II many leaders were called out on to the mission field and it is not surprising that groups started around the world. In addition to these missionaries, after World War II, many Crusaders also found work abroad particularly in the Colonies and so there were many ex-patriot groups of British families. By 1946 there were Crusader groups in Cairo, Jerusalem, and Loka in the Sudan. Sadly, with countries becoming independent, many of the groups closed and the ex-patriots returned to Britain but the work overseas and the links overseas have been retained.

* * *

The rise and fall of a Crusader pianist

David Boulton

(Reprinted with permission from *"The Trouble with God"* by David Boulton, O Books, 2005)

When my brother Brian and I outgrew the Baptist Sunday School at Ashford, Middlesex, immediately after the Second World War, we joined the local Crusaders.

This was a union of Bible classes, originally admitting only public school boys, as there were thought to be plenty of missions to the lower classes but none suitable for those of higher social standing. (There was a Crusaders Union for girls, too, but this split over the theological question of whether or not the girls should be allowed to wear lipstick. Mother was against lipstick – but even more against prohibiting it as a necessary condition of salvation). Brian and I made it into Crusaders by virtue of passing the 11-plus and going to Hampton Grammar School. Occasionally the rules of admitting only public school boys were relaxed, as happened when my father remonstrated with George Lane, our Crusader leader, for refusing membership to the academically challenged son of the local pet shop owner. There was no class system in heaven, he argued, so why have one here below?

The Crusaders movement was strongly Bible-based and evangelical, but non-denominational. The Plymouth Brethren [in which we were brought up] disapproved of our attending, as we risked contamination by Error, but my father and mother stood firm. Classes were held on Sunday afternoons in a dilapidated house in Church Road, Ashford, which was literally falling down around us. One Sunday we noticed that the piano, energetically pounded by chorus master Eddie Fifield, was swaying up and down like a see-saw. The floor beneath it had broken away from its pinning and was springing like a trampoline. No-one thought to organise repairs, and Eddie continued to rise and fall for many a Sunday afternoon, till one day the adjoining lavatory disappeared into the basement, after which it was thought prudent to contact the landlord before the piano and Eddie followed it into the bottomless pit. The landlord was a local speculator who was only waiting for the roof to fall in before demolition and redevelopment. It was a race between the rupture and the Rapture.

What we enjoyed most about Crusaders, apart from the bouncing piano and the disappearing toilet, was summer camps. Every year we joined fellow Crusaders from all over the country, pitching our tents in wonderful farmland sites at Polzeath, Cornwall, or Studland Bay, Dorset. Camp games, camp fires and camp grub were interspersed with Bible readings and emotional invitations to "give your hearts and lives to Christ". I did so – every year. Mine was the most given-away heart in Ashford: I couldn't resist. So every summer's-end I returned home re-renewed and re-redeemed, and sometimes it lasted a whole week. But by the time school term began again I was scrimping on my homework and hoping the unaccountably delayed Rapture would get me off the hook.

* * *

Anecdotes from the Wessex area in the late 1960s

Geoffrey Williams

I was a leader of the Dorchester class from 1968-1972. We strove to become the biggest class in the area but could never overtake Monkton Coombe class which was based at the school of that name. We later discovered the reason – allegedly, if you didn't go to Crusaders, you did extra prep!

As an Education Officer for the County Council, I was required to visit various local schools. On visiting one of the classes of a local church junior school I saw that the children had completed a survey to discover the different churches that they attended, they had displayed their results on a pie chart. The largest slice of the pie by a long way was the one labelled "Crusaders"!

We had an annual picnic on the beach at Durdle Door, the amazing rock arch around the corner from Lulworth Cove. A great long fire was built between parallel baulks of timber and on each side a long line of youngsters lying on their tummies and holding out sausages on sticks to the blaze. Doubtless the risk assessors would have ruled this kind of fun as well out of order if the protection industry had got under way by then!

And finally I remember the wonderful team of leaders of the Dorchester classes – both the boys' and the girls' groups. Foremost among them was Graham Stevens, who is still active as a founding trustee of the 'Dorcas' project which has been bringing new hope and a new life to so many young people in the Philippines.

*   *   *

The Warrington Venture

Keith and Jill Sharman

It was the last Sunday in June 1959 that I said goodbye to my friends at the Banstead class with an average attendance of 80 boys aged 7 to 18 years old. A week later I had moved to my first job near Warrington (a little town halfway between Manchester & Liverpool!)

Warrington Crusaders met in a suburb called Stockton Heath on the south side of the town in the local British Legion Hall at 3.30pm on a Sunday afternoon with attendance of approx 15 from local secondary schools – quite a contrast to Banstead. I spent the following weeks and months making personal visits to homes of possible new members, given to me by existing members. This visiting was very time consuming, but the Lord rewarded our perseverance as a few new faces appeared at steady intervals. Jill & I helped the longer term growth with the unexpected arrival of our twins Richard & Paul, and Martin two years later! A number of the members grew up through the class into Leadership roles later, and Neil Turton, one of these first new members, eventually ended up going into the Anglican ministry.

After a change of meeting venue with a 12.10pm start (to avoid clashing with local Church Sunday Schools), numbers continued to increase, helped by a national competition, based on areas, with a shield given to the class that showed the greatest percentage increase over a certain period – Warrington South (renamed after the formation of the Warrington Culcheth group north-east of the Town) duly won the North West shield. Much of the credit for the Class's outreach and activities must go to my co-leaders Andrew & Bruce Grahame, Peter Hill, Bryan Stone, Ray Crossan, Graham Barwick and others.

At Class Birthday weekends, we held a Parents' Dinner the evening before, at which well known speakers in Crusader circles, such as Jack Watford and Randle Manwaring, introduced Crusader films depicting our many activities. One year about 25 members and Leaders decided to visit the Camp Rally in Westminster Hall in London, but the country was in the grip of big freeze. However we set off on a slow journey, with an impromptu breakfast mid-morning in the train restaurant and eventually arrived at the Rally during the tea interval to a great reception from the other attendees. We soon decided that we should make an early start to our return journey, and arrived back in Warrington about midnight in a ghost train – it was completely covered in hoar frost!

In the mid 60's the leaders considered the formation of a Girls class, which became possible when Jill and I moved to a large Victorian house with outbuildings suitable for

Keith and Jill Sharman

Crusader use. After much prayer and a contact with an ex-Crusader from Manchester, a team of ladies (Daphne Hall, Audrey Stringer & Anthea Hill) agreed to establish this group. Within a year or so a Crusader Fellowship for older members started to meet monthly in our house, and it was truly thrilling to see young people sitting (some on the floor) listening to the Scriptures being expounded by local Christian men & women as well as some from Manchester & Liverpool – you could hear a pin drop, such was the attention!

In the early 1970's the Warrington South class made great use of the Cae Canol Centre in North Wales, and one year took two weekends in September, such was the demand. It was the second weekend that the class achieved its best ever attendance of 106. However from this peak numbers declined a little – so the Leaders decided that if young people would not come to Crusaders we would take Crusaders to them! In 1973 a new group was established for 9.30am on Sunday mornings in Grappenhall – some 2 miles further up the Manchester Ship Canal – with a first meeting attendance of 32 with some initial help from the seniors of Warrington South class. The Warrington Grappenhall group maintained its attendance levels for several years, with help from my co-leaders Norman Harrison, Ray Crossan & Rodger Locke. In the late 1970's we held a class camp for a couple of years at the Crusaders Union site at St David's in South Wales.

After the success of this outreach to Grappenhall, a move was made to establish in 1975 a further group at Lymm (some 5 miles towards Manchester), this time a mixed group at 3pm on a Sunday afternoon. Much support was forthcoming from the elders at Lymm Baptist Church, and this group continued for a number of years with initial help from my wife Jill, Harry & Lois Tickle, Shirley & Peter Rowson, Margaret Stead and others.

With our sons away at University, Jill & I felt it was time to downsize and move nearer our employments in Liverpool and Birkenhead. In mid 1980 we moved to the Wirral.

In summary, as we look back on these twenty years we are truly grateful to the Lord for His blessing and encouragement in the work. We believe that the appeal of Crusaders was greatly enhanced by its sporting activities, with the local classes involved with National Football & Rugby Sevens tournament as well as Merseyside athletics and swimming activities, which in later years became dominated by the Warrington Classes. Through this venture, many young people heard the Gospel with subsequent commitments to Christ as Lord and Saviour. Praise His Name.

*   *   *

Harrogate Crusader Class

Henrik Murden

I was a member of Harrogate Crusader Class in the 1940's. The leader was Mr R.O. King. He was a quiet, sincere person who helped us teenagers grow up in wartime days and afterwards. The Yorkshire class met during the summer at Wetherby; the classes I recall were Leeds Headingly; Leeds Roundhay, and Bradford, but there may well have been more. We played PODEX – a very simple past time.

I went to a Crusader camp at Red Wharf Bay in August 1948. I was in Tent 13 with Tent Officer Mr Thomas The other members of that tent were Alan Beebee from

Walsall; Peter Searle from Upper Tooting; P. Shepherd from New Oscott in Sutton Coldfield; S.Winnick and J Wray of Liverpool Central. These two were the jokers of the tent! The other tent leaders were; Bryan Batten; B.Platt; J.Taylor; Noreen Miller; Ida Thomas; Doris Fairley to name just a few.

Even after all these years the gentleman I remember best was Anthony A. Bentall. I feel he was the person in overall control. It was a well run camp and we had a great time.

Harrogate Crusader class was a great help to me. The Crusader Magazine a good read and without the Crusaders I would not have developed as I did. Hebrews 12 verse 2 was and still is a great inspiration.

*   *   *

Mill Hill Crusaders

Jim Samson

It's been a long journey, but I've never forgotten those Friday evenings and Sunday afternoons at Mill Hill Crusaders in North West London (about 1964 – 67). I went to Mill Hill Crusaders when I was 13 because a boy at school asked me to. You went in past a gleaming black Norton motorcycle parked in the overgrown front garden and into the rooms of what I think was an ordinary suburban house. Many a game of ping pong and then Bible study followed. I honestly believe I learnt to think and argue in the amazingly open debates that sprang into life from the pages of the Bible. As well as Bible study, I went camping for the first time ever, went to Scotland where we tried and failed to cook haggis on an open fire and cycled around France and Switzerland and Ireland with Crusaders. We went to Duffield in Derbyshire many times sleeping on the church hall floor in between getting very wet in the Peak District. Oh yes, many happy memories!

I didn't give my life to Jesus then, although I tried. There must have been other plans for me. I went off onto the usual teenage ways, then University and a job. Perhaps all that was left at that stage was a sense of right and wrong, because I have always tried, with the help of a good wife, to walk the straight and narrow path. I joined a Quaker meeting, which must have been at God's calling and have gained a lot of spiritual sustenance from belonging there.

Fast forward to Cumbria a few years ago and a visit to a village hall where I saw a Crusader shield on the wall. This must have been the first time in 35 years that I can recall seeing one. Amazingly, two of the leaders were present to talk about Crusaders and I wondered at what all this meant. There was no direct link between this event and my attending an Alpha course, but I did and came to experience Jesus in my fifties. Some seeds take a very long time to germinate, but unless they are sown, nothing will grow!

* * *

Oily Fish And Oiled Hair

Pam Pointer

Member of North Harrow CUGA class from 1950s; Leader of Pinner CUGA in the early 1970s. Now Associate/Ex-leader in contact.

Crustless dainty sandwich triangles filled with fish paste... strange fare for strapping lads about to enter manhood? But they went down a treat at Seniors' Teas in a London suburb in the late 1950s. To this 8 year old observer the young gentlemen who filed into our dining room 'after Class' were an awesome sight: tall, soberly-clad in grey flannel trousers with sleek hair oiled closely to their scalps… They were earnest-looking, deep-voiced and ultra-polite (apart from the odd boisterous rogue who'd break a chair or crack a joke).

They sat on upright chairs, knees together, feet apart, toes turned in, carefully balancing a plate on their knees while holding a china cup and saucer. Would the home-made coconut pyramid get into that man's mouth without the cherry rolling down his tie…? Would lurid pink and yellow crumbs from the Battenberg cake add to the more muted specks of colour in his neighbour's tweed jacket…? Would any of them notice that the jelly in little orange glass bowls was made up of different colours and flavours…?

I, a little girl in a man's world, observed it all keenly as my younger brother and I sat in a corner nearly out of sight, certainly out of the minds of the big boys…

Every Sunday Dad, with small leather briefcase, set off shortly after 2 o'clock for the school round the corner to wait for the onslaught of boys who would arrive for the 3 o'clock Crusader class. I went to the Girls' class further up the road but was back in time to help Mum put the jelly in the glasses.

Seniors' Teas didn't happen every week. On 'ordinary' Sundays when Dad came home he immediately sat down, clicked open his case and got out two contrasting books: the Signing-On-Book and the Register. With pencil in hand he entered a dot for an absence or a tiny vertical stroke for attendance against each name in the Register. The other book was much more interesting. Each week he chose a colour picture to stick on the left hand page with suitable caption and Bible verse. On the right hand page the boys signed their names in large scrawl, often incomprehensible, sometimes with assumed names – Charlie Chaplin, Jimmy Greaves, and Colin Cowdrey – but interpreted correctly by the knowing leader. Each week numbers were carefully added up and if the attendance record was broken, the following Sunday a black vinyl record would be smashed ceremoniously.

Crusaders was an integral part of family life. My parents' example of commitment, hospitality and service was as influential as anything I learnt from attending Crusaders myself. The Badge was important, the Bible paramount, the sandwiches and coconut pyramids vital. All contributed to the composite picture that fuelled body, mind and soul then – and for a future generation. What's changed? Probably only the fish paste...

*   *   *

Wallington Crusaders 1945-1955 – and beyond

Geoffrey and Anthony Smith

It was among the biggest news of the week: 'Last Sunday's attendance was 201 and we were top class in the Union. Sutton came second with 199.' Or, of course, the numbers might be the other way round! Competition at Wallington with neighbours Sutton Crusaders for biggest attendance was intense! Dad introduced me to Wallington Crusaders when I was 8 years old; my brother Geoffrey joined at the same age three years later. For the next ten years we hardly missed a Sunday afternoon.

What memories abound from those years! Our leader in Juniors was 'Bishop' Stanley Coates with various co-leaders. He had a great ability to bring Bible events to life for us. Vernon Hedderly, Derrick Lewin, Noel carpenter and others led us during our 'difficult' teenage years in Inters at a time when for us camps became a major part of Crusader life. Each Whitsun there was the Wallington and Beddington camp at Gomshall, near Guildford, at the foot of the North Downs. Remember the Podex and rounders, campfires and singsongs, the old bell-tents and the meeting marquee, Derrick Lewin as

Commie, the lady cooks with Noel Carpenter as Adjy; and the fine teaching, well tailored to our needs.

In the summer we valued the national camps. Bembridge, Polzeath, Stoke Fleming and Studland spring to mind. There was no opportunity for travel abroad in those days, but Cornwall and Dorset seemed exotic enough!

Throughout those years we were treated to excellent Bible teaching, and were encouraged to read a passage of Scripture every day, usually with the Scripture Union notes: daily Bible reading became a habit for life. The habit was strengthened when we went up to Seniors and were allowed into the sanctum of the Senior Hall, with its photograph of King George Vth (in its frame surmounted by the crown) and the inscription "He read his Bible every day". Here our leaders were Mr T.B.Smith, Mr Don Reidpath and HVH, Vernon Hedderly's father.

We enjoyed visiting speakers and visiting missionaries too. There was always a strong missionary emphasis at Crusaders, led by Vernon Hedderly with reports and occasional visits from 'our own missionaries', Arthur Vine (India), Leonard Street (China), Ernest Bawtree (Africa) and later Ken Kitley (Central Africa). Since then, several others have been added to the numbers – including John Chambers (South America), Peter Empson (Crusoe's own roving missionary), Peter Bissett and ourselves.

I had known Jesus as my personal Saviour from very early childhood. At the age of 12 at a camp at Bembridge, I remember wanting to respond to an invitation at the close of a talk, but knew I had already given my life to Jesus. Commie helped the youngster with great kindness, as I remember, to re-commit my life to Him. Years later, as tent Officer at another Gomshall camp, I had the privilege of doing much the same for another young man, Neil Rogers, now in Uzbekistan as an ophthalmic surgeon and the Lord's ambassador.

We, Geoffrey and Anthony, both went abroad as missionaries, he to Papua-New Guinea and (much later) to Israel. I with my wife, Sheila, served as a doctor in Nazareth, North India and Zaire in central Africa with the Baptist Missionary Society between 1964 and 1975.

Looking back 60 years to that first Crusader Sunday afternoon, I am so grateful to God for all that Crusaders taught us of the Lord, of a deep love for the Scriptures, and of the challenge of missionary service. Returning from Zaire, I continued in medicine and became an orthopaedic surgeon. For the last twenty years I have been a hospice doctor in the U.K.

Geoffrey worked for the Commonwealth Secretariat, then for the Imperial Cancer Relief Fund and later joined the pastoral team of a big London church. For the last 15 years he has been working with the Church's Ministry to the Jews, then Prayer for Israel, and latterly for Christian Friends of Israel. With our wives we have taken part in many teaching trips abroad and have been privileged to continue in the service of the Lord Jesus. I value my continuing link with Crusader Associates.

*   *   *

Wallington 1960s

Geoff Lambert
Member and leader of Wallington Class 1946 – 1969.
Very involved with Broads camps and the Seamanship Cruises.
Member of Wellesley Fellowship in 1950's &1960's.
Leader at Birmingham Erdington 1969 – 1979.
Leader of "Crufel" – Crusader Fellowship - Bristol 1979 – 1983.

During the late '60s when I was leader of the seniors at Wallington class, I became very conscious that the Crusader

Hall was not the ideal place for seniors to have discussions. I felt it would be good for us to meet at my flat and to finish with tea before some of us went on to church.

The problem was whether the other leaders would be happy to have the seniors taken away, rather than all meet together, and so it was with some misgivings that I went to Cru's next Sunday to raise the matter.

As soon as I arrived, the senior leader, Derek Lewin, came up to me saying he wanted to see me to discuss something. The Class was thinking of forming an extra section, but the only place to meet would be in the room the seniors used, would I consider taking the seniors to my flat and meeting there?

Needlessly to say we did and it worked wonderfully

*   *   *   .

The 'Damascas' Road

Leslie Baalham

Being a Christian is not just a matter of believing in our heads... doubts we may have... John the Baptist certainly expressed his when the going was tough – 'are you the Christ or should we look for another?'

Job could say I know that my redeemer lives. I want to say that I thank God this has been my experience. As a young man of 16, one Sunday afternoon in a Crusader Bible class I came to realise my personal need of God's forgiveness and my need for a relationship with Jesus. Formal religion has its place, but how much better to be able to say Paul wrote to the young Timothy... 'I know whom I have believed.'

Presented with the facts of the Gospel story I realised being a Christian was more than going to church. God calls for the surrender of our will; it's an invitation for Jesus to take over. That day was my Damascus Road; an encounter with Jesus that has stayed with me through the years, I have let the Lord down time and again, but he has never let me down with his forgiving love.

*   *   *

Ealing Common Crusaders

Jane Eastgate

I was first invited to Ealing Common Crusaders by the lady whose garden we backed onto (Dorothy Ryan) in about 1949. I thank God for that invitation that led onto so much.

Already regularly attending St Peter's Church, Ealing, with my family, Crusaders gave me that added enthusiasm to follow Jesus as a personal Saviour and to sincerely give my life to Him, starting as a Sunday school teacher.

The first great impact was the incentive to attend for ten consecutive Sundays to win our Crusader badge (and oh! how proud I was to wear it every day), then for 25 Sundays to obtain our New Testament engraved with a Crusader badge on the front cover, still so treasured today; and then the biggest prize to work for, after 50 Sundays was my handsome 'Knighthood Bible' which, alas, has now worn out with use, having been read, studied, marked and transported to church services, meetings, Crusader camps and Christian conferences.

Finally to top them all, was the much longed for framed picture 'Follow Me' of Jesus leading children of all nationalities along a road, which was awarded to the person who had brought the most new people during the year. A great idea!

The other lasting impact and happy memory were the wonderful Easter Crusader camps at Oakdene School at Beaconsfield, Wisper's School at Midhurst and St Christopher's, Horsham where it was brought home to us strongly that Jesus died for us personally and loved us as individuals, inviting our response to His challenge.

That has stayed with me and led me onto Christian witness at school, starting a Scripture Union group, into Nursing training at the Middlesex Hospital, London, and then to marrying our church's curate and sharing enthusiastically in parish and Vicarage life and witness for 40 years. Now in semi-retirement, I'm a Marie Curie nurse in people's own homes, also helping in voluntary church work with the under 5's services, and with bereaved people (visiting and running groups).

That early Christian motivation and enthusiasm from Crusaders has meant so much and proved so valuable, and will stay with me for life! I am so thankful.

*   *   *

On Route to Dormansland...

David Wheble

Meeting the Carpenter of Nazareth as a teenager changed my life forever! All through the 120 strong boys Crusaders at Hayes, Kent; Camping at Woolacombe, special events at Easter like trips to Hovis and Payne's Chocolates, but with a BYOG tea and lively meeting to follow are some of the highlights I recall.

Hitchin group was next, headed up by Leslie Newth, Barry Turner and Flt. Lt. Probert. The leaders involved me in all sorts of things including leading Juniors on occasions and even a first preach at 16! That was scary!! The next step was with Kelvinside, Glasgow whilst at Bible College, an excellent group with a very good leadership especially one whose wife taught domestic science and at whose home I first took a liking to cauliflower cheese.

Bexleyheath Group with Neville Jennings, Alan and David Shelley followed, with Sir Cliff Richard speaking at one of the birthdays and with excellent parental support. Soon a new girls group started with Kathleen Fawcett and my wife Ruth, later to merge with us boys. Carrying 11 in our Renault 16 from a local estate was fun but another leader did buy a minibus later! Events like the Masked Masquerade in a farm barn and coming dressed as a 'beautiful' blonde woman, one or two kids thought I was Neville's wife!! I was more worried that I might be stopped in my mini by the police. Trips to Westbrook for the day; the annual Athletics Meeting at Motspur Park and elsewhere, with some success. The New Year annual commissioning service in London was always inspirational.

Then Dormansland village, starting from scratch but with exciting growth to over 130! Night hikes, with one ending up through the grounds of Leeds Castle with a line of ducks and ducklings off the lake crossing our path. Bonfire nights with loads of kids and parents before too many rules and regulations, let alone the galloping costs.

Crusader Holidays, Spree from the outset near Haywards Heath, excellent site and God heard our cry to stop the heavy rain one year to set up the tents and at the end, after the tents were all down a few drops and then on exiting from the site, the heavens opened! Hallelujah! Taking on the leadership of Sandle Manor 1 summer holiday with a fantastic team every year, praise God, amazing fun times with great variety of children, for example the boy who only ate jam sandwiches, and another only mars bars! Swimming every day, a plethora of organised events with and without water! Great chaplains and no pressure commitments and recommitments to Christ which grew each year as we all prayed. Fabulous, exhausting but very memorable!

Above all else, seeing young people give their lives to Christ and going on with Him. It is so exciting to see a Crusader couple both saved through the group now the youth leaders in our current church; others leading children's work, past and present. One now leads the Dormansland Urban Saints group. Ruth and I praise God for such ongoing memories.

*   *   *

Exeter Crusaders

Gerald Nathan Miller

I was 84 in July 2011. Brought up in a Brethren family in Exeter, and from 11 a pupil of Hills School, I joined the local Crusaders about 1940. We met in, or close to, Exeter School where our leader Maurice Stephens was a teacher; other leaders were George Ponsford and Mr Saunders, both masters at Mount Radford School. Two of my close friends were Ernest Holmes and Geoff Philpot, and a third, Russell Fairhead.

We met every Sunday afternoon, and enjoyed singing the choruses and hearing the list read out of attendances at other gatherings the previous week. I think the favourite was Strawberry Hill, somewhere in London, if my memory serves me still.

We used to meet up with the Girl Crusaders two or three times a year; once at the home of Mr and Mrs Percy Sercombe in Pennsylvania – their son, Theodore, and daughter, Joy, were both Crusaders, once over Dartmoor in the summer and always on Boxing Day in Boys v Girls Hockey match. As a 'rugby' boy, and not 'hockey', I never played. One year Theodore was hit by the ball, very painfully, and was attended by Dr Norah Sims, a friend of Mrs Sercombe, as her husband Dr. Charles was serving in the RAMC!

However, after about three years, I was begged by the Superintendent to start Sunday School teaching in a hall in Burnthouse Lane, Exeter, a new (just) pre-war housing estate, where over 250 children gathered Sunday by Sunday. A girl, my age, was trying to cope with 24/25 nine year old girls and I was pressed to take on a dozen of them. It wouldn't be allowed in 2011, would it?

*   *   *

Eastwood Baptist Crusaders

Mike Jeffery

In 1973 the youth group at Eastwood Baptist Church had fallen on hard times – 5 people and things were not looking good. God knew otherwise – he sent two people to Eastwood – Mike Graves and Eve Schooling who were local Crusader leaders.

After not too much persuasion Rob Land and Steve Pearman and I set off to Saffory Close to become leaders at The Eastwood Boys class. It was a two way street – we were leading in Crusaders and many of the older youngsters were coming to Eastwood. Under the strong teaching of Eve and Mike many came to know Jesus as their Saviour. Many of the churches in the Southend-on-Sea area now have deacons, elders and leaders who were grounded first in Crusaders.

Ask me for my memories of Crusaders and my mind races over the 12 years I was actively involved and still now as an Associate Member. Here are a few ·

- Noisy Sunday morning classes with kids we thought were not listening – don't believe it they did and years later it is remembered;

- Crux – once a month for the 14+. Spiritual (yes sometimes), fun always and sometimes plain mad – playing football on the mud flats at Leigh on Sea;

- Norfolk Broads and all the pranks there;

- Sizewell Hall for house parties;

- Conversation between myself and a friend walking through the city – we really enjoyed our teen years;

- Camps at Danbury and elsewhere – officer hunts on a bank holiday afternoon;

- Crusader Sports Days – I am now an Athletics Official!!

There is a huge debt of gratitude owed to those in this area who had the vision for Crusaders including the Scotts, the Bawtrees, Gordon Cooper, Keith McCullough, Wilf and the Amis family to name a few.

My abiding memory of Crusaders is the simplicity of its mission – Church for the unchurched – how many people have grown to know that Christians can enjoy themselves and yet by their example lead others to know Jesus.

*   *   *

Kenton Crusaders

Paul Rose

Realising I joined a Crusader class as a Junior 60 years ago is a bit daunting.

My class was Kenton, East Harrow in the sprawling suburbs of NW London, which I joined in 1951, aged 8. The class ran Juniors at 2.30 followed by Inters and Seniors at 3.30 on Sunday afternoons. On a good day this was followed by tea at a leader's house. We met in the Conservative Hall and our Seniors group met in the party agent's office with pictures of prime ministers Winston Churchill, Harold Macmillan and later Edward Heath on the wall. Yet it was there, we as teenagers were taught the scriptures and my friend Philip, who was doing "classics" at A level used to bring his Greek NT to help us understand what the apostle Paul really meant!

Memories:

Friendly Rivalry: The returns sheets and the rivalry between local groups; our big challenge was to try and be ahead of Finchley or Mill Hill in attendance numbers. Watford, however, was always out of our league!

Friendships and faith building: from a Junior to becoming a leader in my early 20's the Crusader class provided great friendship and wise leaders which were key to my spiritual growth.

Fellowship: Harrow area had a number of classes and the Senior Area Fellowship met monthly on a Saturday night. These brought Seniors and leaders, boys and girls (GCU in those days) for a "squash". Kenton, Harrow, Hatch End, North Harrow, Pinner and Northwood classes were represented.

Fun: Many went to Bembridge in the summer; over the years I headed for Westbrook, Studland, Stoke Fleming,

Polzeath, St David's and Pelistry Bay. We played 'podex' every Wednesday evening in the summer term on the fields next to Northwick Park Metropolitan line station. The area is now a huge hospital site. I was impressed that one of our leaders, a bank manager, sometimes came straight from work in suit and with briefcase (can't remember the bowler hat) to be there. On Whit Mondays we linked up with Chorley Wood and Northwood classes for a games time on Chorleywood common. On New Year's Day we met with local Crusaders for mixed hockey; more dangerous and colder than hacker at Westbrook in the summer.

Foundational: These were times for laying good foundations of faith for life.

*   *   *

Leicester Evington Crusaders

Phillip Hutchinson

My earliest recollection of Crusaders was at Leicester Evington from about 1958 onwards (I was 9 at this year) until that class closed eventually due to lack of leaders. But I also had experience of Leicester Glenfield for a brief period. Sunday (afternoon) classes were the core activity of course, usually at 3pm for about an hour, divided equally between worship and teaching.

My most joyful recollections were singing choruses (I still have my chorus book, as I also still have my Crusader (authorised) Bible dated March 17th 1963), going swimming and playing games during the week, and probably best of all going to Easter house parties where we played weird games such as 'hacker' (nothing to do with computers – a game similar to hockey) and 'crocker' (a game between rounders and cricket but played with a large round ball), and the usual wide game played by the whole crowd. Worship and teaching would be all together and along with eating formed the central activities. It was a great time!

I also remember going to rallies at the Central Hall Westminster for a great all Crusader get-together sometime usually in the early spring as I recollect. The morning would be spent at some activity, like museums or train spotting in London, and the afternoon would be worship, reports from all over England and some refreshments.

There was also a Leicester Athletics meeting where all the Leicester Crusader classes would compete against each other, and there were quite a few in the early 60's, the tug-of-war often being the high light of the afternoon.

I also attended my local parish church, but it is Crusaders that I remember with great fondness for the fellowship, friendship, fun and most importantly, the introduction to the Lord Jesus Christ who through Crusaders became my close friend and personal Saviour for the rest of my life to the present moment.

*　　*　　*

Sidcup Crusaders

Robert Hunt

In 1932, when I was eight years old, I was invited by a school-friend to go to Sidcup Crusaders, in Kent. Its Junior section met in an NBWTAU (National British Women's Total Abstinence Union) hall situated in someone's back-garden.

I was immediately struck by the warm welcome that I received, and thoroughly enjoyed the singing, especially the choruses, and the talks which were always interesting. I can still remember some of those given by a Mr Braby who always brought along a visual aid. The leader was a Captain Downes; one Sunday he said that our group could be divided by a line, that no-one could see, that divided us into those who had accepted Jesus and those who had not. I really wanted to be the right side of that line, and that night before going to sleep I prayed that if I had accepted Jesus I would not have one of those nightmares that had been troubling me recently. When I awoke I realised that I had not had a nightmare, and ever since then I have not doubted that Jesus has saved me.

There followed times in the Intermediate and Senior sections of the class; and, through the mixed fellowship, I met the girl who has now been my wife for 64 wonderful years! Of course, I have let the Lord down many times, but he has enabled me to be a Crusader leader of Sidcup, Harrow, Pinner, and Northwood Hills classes, and two periods of Chairmanship of the General Committee.

Over the years I have attended many Crusader conferences where really helpful teaching and wonderful fellowship were regularly experienced. The local classes in the Harrow area held a series of house parties at Westbrook, on the Isle of Wight, and these were times when lives were dedicated or rededicated to the Lord. More recently, in five successive summers, my wife and I led a mixed work-party at a home for disabled children in Malmesbury; it was great to see the faith of the participants being expressed in such a practical manner.

Crusaders has been the instrument by which God has led many to faith, and I am so grateful for that invitation in 1932 that has led me to so much blessing.

*   *   *

Newcastle-under-Lyme Crusaders

John Butterworth

As a youngster I was brought up in a high Anglican church, but it was Crusaders that showed me that Christianity was fun.

I was a 12-year-old grammar school boy when I was invited by my form teacher and chemistry master, Donovan Lurie, to go along one Sunday afternoon to Newcastle-under-Lyme Crusader class. After two bus rides lasting 40 minutes and a short walk to John Caddick-Adams' large imposing stone house and huge garden I arrived in a large room full of about 70 youngsters. I was relieved to recognise teachers John Ditchfield and John Carr and some older boys from my school.

The afternoon service with modern songs, quizzes and games was totally different to the morning ritual and ceremony that I was accustomed to. I was used to a majestic and distant God, but Crusaders taught me about a Creator who was interested in me personally. With Saturday night games in a nearby school, trips to London on the new 100mph trains and the chance of exciting holidays in Britain and abroad I soon became a regular Crusader. I didn't mind the journeys as I could use the change from the tickets to try each week a different 2oz of sweets from one of the multi-coloured jars that filled the window of the old fashioned shop where the bus stopped.

In Easter 1965 I was invited by the Crusaders leaders, to join Tony Gill from Eastbourne in a holiday in Lucerne, Switzerland. It was so good that my parents let me go the following year to Innsbruck, Austria, where I made my Christian commitment. I tried for a hat-trick in Holland the next Easter, but my parents said two overseas holidays were enough. However they allowed me instead to join a

Crusader holiday camping on St Mary's, Bryher and St Agnes in the Scilly Isles. It seemed the perfect holiday; the sun shone every day and so began a life-long love affair with the islands.

As the years went by I moved up from Juniors to Seniors and then Super Seniors. I tried to explain years afterwards to my wife that super was not my spiritual state but from my classical Latin upbringing of being above in age of the ordinary Seniors.

In the 1980s and now with two young boys my wife and I were invited to join Lawrie Lowton, head teacher of Garforth Comprehensive School, near Leeds, on an annual Crusader camp for 100 pupils, firstly on the Isle of Man, then in North Wales. With 2,000 pupils, Lawrie decided the best way to introduce them to Christianity was through a Crusader class. Life had turned full circle as I again enjoyed the games, the dramas and helped our two young sons on hunt the officer.

Forty-six years later Christianity is still fun, and though I am possibly too old for games and camping I am eternally grateful to Crusaders for starting me out on my spiritual journey.

* * *

Finchley Crusaders

Rev Colin Perkins (retired)

I was a member of Finchley Crusaders from about 1945 to 1959 when I got married. I regularly played the piano for hymns and choruses – Golden Bells and CSSM choruses. I was also an assistant leader. My brother, John Perkins, was an elected leader until he left to get married.

I remember the celebration of our 50th anniversary in about 1957 or 1958 when Herbert Bevington who had founded the Finchley class was present. I remember making the suggestion that he should be asked to present when presentations were made to junior members so that they could recall in 50 years time that they had met Mr Bevington.

Finchley was one of the largest classes. Quite a number of members went on to full-time Christian service. Members included Sir Cliff Richard and Bill Latham.

*   *   *

Birmingham Harborne Crusaders

H Gordon Smith

From around 1945-1953 I went to Birmingham Harborne Crusaders which met in the Dunton Community Centre in Ridgacre Road. My father H.T.W. Smith was one of the leaders, with Stephen Wood. We met at 3pm on Sunday afternoons, and had mid week "Keynites". The Bible teaching on Sundays and the CSSM choruses certainly helped my spiritual development. I was born November 1937, so was part of the class from ages 7–15. The family were Christians, so I also had a good upbringing at Birmingham Harborne Brethren and St Johns Harborne, before starting to attend Friary Road Baptist, Dudley in 1947, by which time we had moved to Selly Park.

The mid week activities included games and model railways (my father was keen on this!). We also had Annual Rallies at the Digbeth Institute, and I remember as speakers Cecil J Allen (who used to organise railway trips for Crusaders, though I did not go on any), and Mr Hunt who worked for Kodak and spoke on how colour film and photos were made. As far as I can recall, we had about 30 in the class.

For about eighteen months in 1967-68 I was assistant

leader at Tettenhall, Wolverhampton under Mr. Webb; by then classes met at 9.30am. I was not involved from 1953-67 for family, medical and National Service reasons, and in 1968 moved to work in London, marrying in 1969, and did not continue my involvement with Crusaders. I enjoyed and benefited from it socially and in a growing understanding of God's Word.

*   *   *

Nairobi Crusaders

Hugh Sansom

I was involved with Nairobi Crusaders from 1951 to 1970. Nairobi Crusaders was under the overall leadership of Dr Fulford Jarvis, a Nairobi GP, and his wife.

Nairobi Crusaders was mainly for pupils at the main boarding schools – Nairobi Primary, the Prince of Wales (Secondary) and the Duke of York (Secondary). These schools were originally for expatriate children but became multi racial after Kenya's Independence. So in the early days, Crusaders was all "white", but became multi-racial in the late 60's.

Those attending Crusaders included many missionary children. In some cases (especially Nairobi Primary – with which I was involved) the schools provided transport to bring the children to Crusaders – so that a time out of school (with refreshments provided as well as the Crusader Bible class) was an added incentive to coming. In the two secondary schools, I think the Crusader class was held in the school. There were also Girl Crusaders for the Primary School and for the (girls) Kenya High School – with which my wife, Sue, helped.

*   *   *

Crouch End 1901

Hendon Class 1915

CHAPTER FOUR

Emerging Leaders

*'There are different kinds of gifts, but the same Spirit.
There are different kinds of service, but the same Lord.
There are different kinds of working, but the same God
works all of them in all men.'*

1 Corinthians 12 v 4-6

There is often comment made about the young people of today becoming the leaders of tomorrow, but should that be young people today becoming the leaders of today? Even back in the early days of Crusaders, leaders recognised this and boys would often be asked to read the Scripture for that day and comment on it, making observations as they saw fit. For many this 'ordeal' became character building and many cite their eventual role in adult life as having its grounding in roles such as this within a group situation.

Training leaders and teachers of the future was what Jesus sought to do with His disciples. Jesus gave his disciples the skills and abilities that they needed to become the early church, evangelists and teachers. When they started out, I guess they wouldn't have dreamed about taking on the roles that they did, as with many who have been in leadership positions and those who remain so today. We often cannot believe that we could ever do or be in a position of responsibility.

Leadership and training of young people remains so critical within Christian youth work, equipping young people to become the people that God created them to be. This is where young people have their values shaped, their knowledge of the Gospel securely grounded, their habits formed and their skills and abilities discovered in save and unthreatening environments.

The work continues, the leaders emerge and take on the role in society that has been God prepared for them.

* * *

The Early Film Maker

Alan Vogt Herne Bay Crusaders/Moseley Crusaders

I've been connected with Crusaders for 64 years and was made a Life Member. I joined Herne Bay Crusaders as a junior in 1935. We evacuated to Birmingham during the war and I linked up with Moseley Crusaders where I was appointed Sunday School Superintendent at our church.

I came to faith in Christ at the age of 14 at a Pioneer house party led by Mr David Tryon who was a 'padre' at Crusader camps. Those camps were great fun and provided great fellowship and training for Christian service. Two months after our wedding, I took my wife, Mary, to camp. Having been cooking for two, she found herself helping to cook for 200!

When I was called up, I was stationed in Portsmouth and so I helped with the Crusaders there. I was then sent to the Army of Occupation in Austria and I met a Crusader in Vienna who linked me up with a Christian dentist in London who was looking for a colleague. On my return to civilian life I joined his practice and got involved in Upper Tooting and Wandsworth Common Crusaders as a leader in the junior section. This class was a flourishing class, one of the oldest in the Union, started in 1909 which has many claims to fame including:

- Many trophies won at the Union Sports Day

- Prize winner for the Union "Make a filmstrip" competition. (We did a modern day version of the prodigal son)

- Took over an edition of the magazine one month.

- Produced Crusader Shield stamps (this was at the time when Green Shield trading Stamps were popular) as incentives to regular attendances and recruiting etc and with stamps taken off a boy's card for bad behaviour!

We had regular evangelistic missions at our Easter camps and the later Class camps at Capel and Fairlight with games by the sea and trips to Hastings.

Jack Watford, Union General Secretary, suggested that it would help to have filmstrips of Crusaders. I said "What a good idea" to which he replied "Go ahead!" I composed filmstrips on *Recruiting, the Badge* and *the history of the Union*. We also had a missionary theme based on the astronauts' link with NASA headquarters – so similarly, we at home should be giving close support to our missionaries. At a leader's conference, I said "I'm dividing the filmstrip into three parts – one of a male missionary, one of a female missionary and one...." Resulting in roars of laughter, wondering what sort of human being the third would be! Actually, I was thinking in terms of a Crusader doing secular work overseas!

I was also on the Crusader Union missionary committee, meeting at the home of Sir Eric and Lady Richardson. When Ernie Addicott left the Mission Aviation Fellowship and became Secretary of Crusaders, he joined this committee. This was at the beginning of short term teams going overseas – one went to Africa to construct a new airstrip.

I am so thankful to the Lord for all my time in Crusaders and glad of this opportunity of an 84 year old to jot down my reminiscences.

Servanthood Taught

David R Ralph, Tunbridge Wells Boys Crusaders

Although over 40 years ago, I can still remember the knock on the front door from two Crusader Leaders inviting me to join the Tunbridge Wells Boys Class; one of the largest in the country. With Christian parents I had always gone to church and been given a solid foundation, but that invitation to Crusaders started something very much more than just believing in God. I am sure resistance would have been pointless as within minutes of a flicker of interest, arrangements were being made to collect and return me home and rapid mention of other activities other than just the Sunday afternoon class which was at 1500 hours prompt.

It was the Leaders on that evening who made a strong impact on me; Leaders who, after a day in London as a commuter, would be out knocking on doors to invite someone they did not know to Crusaders.

The Sunday class went on to give me a biblical grounding and a stronger faith but it also taught me much more in that everyone should serve in some way, and then went on to provide the opportunities for us to do so. It is a lesson which has stayed with me, because the leaders were always there for us, but most importantly they demonstrated both their faith and service in all they did and as we got older they mentored us in the roles they had got us to take on.

These were not men without other responsibilities and

would have been shocked to hear the words "Work Life Balance" as they gave 100% to everything they did. This was particularly shown by three Leaders, initially, who were also teachers and hence seen in action both at School & Crusaders. At the time they seemed "old" but looking back they were mainly newly qualified teachers making their way in careers as well as giving as much as they did to Crusaders. By today's standards many would consider them fanatics; Monday nights were leaders meeting, mid week was spent visiting, Friday Night was Bible Study, there was a Saturday Activity and then the Sunday Class (when did they prepare?) but it built relationship and service.

They introduced me to both residential events, including the gem of Westbrook, including leadership training, all of which have stayed with me all my life. Because they showed a chance to see the "real" leader & their faith at all times of the day and so often the night too! Although running our own local House party, each Easter there was always full promotion of the national events; to which we were taken at least once a term and "Summer Camp" – no one dared miss the January closing date as it was an almost certainty then to miss out on your first choice camp that summer. Not being a fan of canvas, but not being able to escape from attending something, they got me to go for a House party and even more of a surprise one of the very few mixed ones – as always looking forward & not behind in what should be happening.

These were my Crusader Leaders of old a most welcome bread; faithful to the local class, the national organisation & most of all to individuals like me.

*   *   *

Reality Christianity

Geoff Mason, Watford Crusaders

Ray Bywaters was the first person I met linked to Watford Crusaders. He often spent time amongst the train spotters on the footpath near Watford Junction that overlooked the four lines going North West. I was one of those train spotters and he chatted to me on a number of occasions. But it was actually through a fellow 12 year old called Ron Howse in my grammar school class that I first went along to the Sunday afternoon meetings. He invited me along, and it was the start of many years of contact with leaders and others who I came to respect and appreciate. They personified Christianity for me. It was so very different to the Sunday School classes that had been my previous experience. The leaders like Ray, were fun, yet had a living faith that informed their actions and behaviour. I wanted to be like them and became a Christian at 13 (in 1956) as a result of a Dick Rees special campaign one Easter.

Earning my badge (10 attendances), getting my Knighthood Bible (52 attendances), learning Bible verses, going on outings, going to West Herts Crusader Camp all came as part of the package. I enjoyed the competitive nature of the Sunday afternoons, as well as the singing of choruses. There were also Bible studies during the week (called Keenites!) where looking at particular passages in depth taught me how much there was in them.

The camp experience was also great fun. I was able to be on holiday with contemporaries and do the things boys like doing. Swimming, podex, football, table tennis, Crocker and halo all featured. Wide games were another regular. Living with these Christian leaders for a week or longer enabled me to see that their Christianity was like seaside rock, "printed all through"; it wasn't just put on for a couple of hours on a

Sunday. In due course, I became one of those camp officers, including being the Quartermaster for a camp of 150.

Leaving home as a 17 year old to work in Coventry for a year before going to Birmingham University, it was Crusader leaders in that city who provided a welcoming link for me and introduced me to young people and churches there.

Many years later I was able to give something back when my wife and I led three summer residential house parties (for Pathfinders through, rather than Crusaders). And that in turn led on to me taking on the full-time job heading up the camps and house parties programme for CPAS for 9 years. My experience in Crusaders as a boy convinced me of the tremendous opportunities that such residential experiences provide.

I shall be eternally grateful for the effective ministry of Crusaders and its major influence on me.

*   *   *

A Theme of Sport and I was Hooked …

Ian Lancaster, Bass Lake Crusaders

Currently Youth Team Leader – Christians in Sport

Only the other day whilst moving house, rooting through some old boxes I came across the Crusader badge – still pinned to the card that describes its meaning; and the memories came flooding back!

During the Spring of 1990 I was invited by a friend to come along to their youth group. "You'll love it" he said. And so on that Thursday evening I jumped on his school bus to his home and on another 15 miles in his car with my friend's father to the Bass Lake Crusader group in the heart of the Lake District. My friend was right – I did love it, and looking back now I loved it for 3 reasons:

The Activities: I can remember on that very first night getting a sheet of paper describing every week right up until the summer holidays – Football, Wide Games, BBQ, Football, Canoeing, Midnight Walk, Football, Rock-climbing, Orienteering, Lads v Dads Football, Community Project, weekend away at Birmingham (National Football Tournament). When a boy of 13 reads a list like that, he gets excited! It was great fun – it was the first time that I had attempted many of the activities and seeing that the theme of football ran from beginning to end, I was hooked from the beginning!

The Group: It was a mix of older and younger lads but there seemed to be a unity in the group that drew me in. I felt at home. Everyone wanted to be there, there was a real buzz and excitement about the group and it was infectious. I guess it was the camaraderie and the banter – doing boy things, with a group of boys – we were on one big adventure, growing up into young men.

The Leaders: We had 4 committed leaders – Terry, Chris, Gordon and John. They were family men and they knew what boys our age wanted. They got stuck into all the activities – they were one of us and looking back now I hugely respected them. I felt loved, I felt cared for, I felt looked after and at the time we took it all for granted. But it wasn't just how they were that was striking; it was what they taught us. Every evening we would have a short epilogue, usually at the end. They were some of the first people who told me about Jesus – They taught us Galatians 2 v20 and we learnt it as a memory verse. I was intrigued. I wasn't a Christian, in fact I didn't become a Christian until my last year of University but I know that wonderful seeds of the glorious Gospel message were planted in my life during my Crusader years – and I'll be forever grateful!

'Ste Braithwaite' – Thanks for being a great friend and inviting me to your Crusader group – I'm certain it has played a big part in shaping me and the memoires are tremendous!

A Call To Go…

Charles and Enid Pocock, Worthing Crusaders

Our introduction to and involvement with Crusaders was also that to the foreign mission field. I was attending Worthing Crusaders at the earlier part of the war until I was called up. It was there that I was invited to join The League of Pioneers, the Junior branch of the South Africa General Mission (SIM) by one of the senior members. We prayed, wrote letters and gave to the support of missionaries in Mozambique.

When in Rhodesia (Zimbabwe) while in training to be an RAF pilot, I met missionaries, who while praying for me, spoke prophetically that I would be returning to Africa as a missionary! My interest and part confirmation of this came, when one Sunday evening, while attending the service at the Baptist Church in Salisbury (Harare), the missionaries we had prayed for while at the Class in Worthing turned up! We were each surprised to meet, even though, for them, it was also a sad occasion as they had come to bury one of their colleagues who had died of Malaria. Seven years later, my wife and I arrived on the same mission station in Mozambique, having been specifically called to "GO" and the SAGM having the confirmation of sending us there on account of both my previous encounter with the Mission and the missionaries. At our valedictory service members of the Worthing Crusaders Adventure Club presented me with a large Crusader plaque which faces me on the wall even as I now write! It was a great encouragement to know that the Class would be supportive.

My wife's involvement with the Girls Crusaders was through the Lone Crusaders' leader in Preston whom she had met and through whose encouragement to read and study the Bible, became a believer. It was through a keen missionary minded NYLC group in Blackpool that she had sensed the call to missionary work about which we had often written while I was serving overseas. We both received the confirmation of our earlier calls together two weeks after we were married while attending the first of the Missionary Conventions at the Holand Road Baptist Church in Hove! Several years later while on furlough she was a guest at an Annual Girls' Crusader Rally in London where she was introduced as Crusaders' first "Lone Crusader" to go as a missionary!

Crusaders was not only a formative force in our earlier lives but one for which we have had cause to thank God for the encouragement we have received through continuing links on many occasions. When leaving for active service, I was given a list of names of Crusaders abroad and was welcomed into their homes for fellowship (and food!) while both passing in transit in Durban and while stationed in Salisbury.

We have not lost our enthusiasm for Crusaders and much encouraged as we continue daily to pray and praise God for the growth and development of the Groups especially in the area of the City of Brighton and Hove where we now live.

* * *

Conversion and Call

David Evans, Finchley Crusaders

It was Easter 1936. I was a boy of ten years old and I was standing at the door of a church hall in Finchley. If I wasn't panting, I had just stopped because I had come on the run.

The compulsion I felt to be there that night was the result of the night before. The Crusader class I attended was holding a week long evangelistic Campaign and Captain Reginald Wallis was the evangelist. The first night I was gripped by the message and came away with the overwhelming conviction that I was not a Christian. Reasonably good I might be; religious to a certain extent I was; but if that was what was involved in being a Christian, I was not. This powerful negative conviction had its positive reaction. I must return the next evening and become a Christian; hence the eager breathless figure at the door.

As I stood there I talked to myself. "As I go into this hall, I know I am not a Christian. I am not coming out until I know I am." Then I added this, "And when I am preaching in the days to come, I shall be able to use this as an illustration – I went in knowing I am not a Christian; I came out knowing I am." So I pulled myself up to my full height and took my place with the other boys who made up the audience.

Captain Wallis spoke on the new birth from the familiar chapter in John's gospel. The key to the new life, the real Christian life I was seeking, was in "the birth from above." The message was crystal clear, "You must be born again." I bowed my head and responded to the invitation. As the meeting came to a close, the speaker asked those who had so responded to tell their leader. With some trepidation I crept up alongside mine and blurted out the words, "I have been born again." His response was loud and clear, "Praise the Lord!" I just about fell through the floor with embarrassment but at the same moment my heart was filled with "joy unspeakable and full of glory."

Some months later I was in the neighbouring suburb of Golders Green at what we called a Squash. The speaker was the well-known Montague Goodman. He showed slides, of children's meetings he had held on some of the beautiful beaches in South Africa. I heard the Lord telling me, "That is where you are going for Me." For me it was the call of God and, as it proved to be, the revelation of a destiny. I served in Southern Africa with the South Africa General Mission (later the Africa Evangelical Fellowship) for some forty years.

The words still sound in my heart. "You must be born again. God called me by His grace… so that I might preach Him…" I am so thankful that Crusaders was so meaningfully involved.

* * *

Tent Maker, Teacher and Leader

Eddie James
Letchworth / Sunderland / Welwyn Garden City / Hatfield Crusaders

After joining Crusaders at the age of 13 we had a visiting speaker who presented the gospel. I made a deal with God to become a Christian for one week to see how things went! That decision transformed my life and 52 years later I am still and always will be a Christian.

Over the years I have been privileged to be involved in Crusaders both as a member of Letchworth Crusaders (1953 – 1958) and in leadership at Sunderland Crusaders (1968 – 1970), Welwyn Garden City Crusaders (1970 – 1977) and Hatfield Crusaders (1977 – 1984).

Residential activities have also played their part within my ministry both in the UK and abroad most recently CRUSoe to South India in 1993 and 1994.

I am grateful to Crusaders for having a large part to play in preparing me for my three vocations that have run in parallel and often merged:

- "tent maker" missionary, my "tent making" was civil engineering and grass roots development in Africa, Asia, Middle East, Far East and the Caribbean.

- mountaineer/ outdoor adventure leader

- teacher in universities and Crusader groups and camps

I am now working part time for Christian Vision for Men and Christian Aid.

Looking back on five decades of being a Crusader I want to thank God for all the folk who have discipled me, many have been younger in the faith than me. Remember Christian maturity is not how long you have been a Christian or how old you are but how close your walk with God is.

* * *

From Boyhood to Young Manhood

David Stuckey, Yeovil Crusaders

I didn't know it at the time, but I'd reached a crossroads, and my life was about to take an exciting new turn, and go up a gear.

All through my years at primary school I had attended a Baptist church with my parents, and gone through the Sunday School system. Now I had passed my 11-Plus and was at the Grammar School, Sundays increasingly seemed to belong to my past rather than my future. I needed to grow, in more ways than one.

Then a friend suggested Crusaders. The class met on Sunday afternoons in a local school hall and I instantly fitted in. It was like someone had switched on a light in my life, enabling me to enter a world of new experiences.

The leader was a local businessman called Lionel Nichols, but everyone, even his wife, seemed to call him Nick. He held 'KeyNite' Bible studies at his home on Friday evenings; he took us in his capacious Armstrong Siddeley to play 'puddox' (I never did know how to spell it!) against boys from other youth clubs in the surrounding villages; we were introduced to the outdoor fun of the 'Sausage Sizzle' (nothing quite so fancy as a barbecue but we loved it).

Sunday afternoons were geared at our level – choruses, Bible readings, talks ... all were pertinent and personal, not patronizing. Nick and his team had that teenage touch which fired our imaginations.

When I received my Knighthood Bible, it was from Sir Alfred Owen, a Crusader patron and at that time head of the Rubery Owen manufacturing group. His firm was also one of the sponsors of the BRM motor racing team. It gave me an added thrill to shake the hand of a man who had shaken hands with one of my boyhood heroes – the racing driver Graham Hill!

In time I was encouraged to attend Crusader camp at St David's and Westbrook, returning as a tent leader (I spent the afternoon as a pair of Wellington boots under a bemused farmer's Land Rover while the other lads tried to find me – and while the farmer's very young daughter occasionally assaulted my shins with a wrench while I pretended to fix her father's exhaust pipe!)

What did Crusaders do for me? It helped me grow up – it was an essential part of my transition from boyhood to young manhood. Everyone treated me not as a child but as an equal. I learnt respect and responsibility. I no longer spoke and thought as a child.

And so in time, through the witness and the word at Crusaders, I gladly made a commitment to Christ, and I always look back on that period with affection and gratitude.

Field Days (and Years) in Crusaders

Rev Brian and Peter Field
Leeds Roundhay / Alwoodley / Headingley Crusaders

On a Sunday morning in January 1944, I was out walking our dog, Pluto, when I met John and Leigh Holmes who were school friends and they told me about Crusaders and I promised to go the next week. I kept my promise and found that Roundhay Crusaders met in the bar of the Conservative Club. I was given a warm welcome and, despite the religious element, I attended regularly, enjoying the games and outings. I went to camps and house parties and again enjoyed the games and the fun, but sat through the meetings not really listening.

In August 1945 I went to Beaumaris Camp, having made up my mind that I would not disrupt the meetings but that the message would "go in one ear and out of the other". On the Sunday we didn't play games but went to the local English-speaking Church with a very Welsh preacher. He spoke on John 9 v 29 "One thing I know, I was blind but now I see". God spoke to me through that man and that Scripture and I gave my life to Christ at the age of fourteen. I even attended the open-air meeting in the town that night..

I encouraged my younger brother, Peter, to join Crusaders and two years later, at Blair Atholl Camp, he, too, gave his heart to Christ. We were both railway enthusiasts and from then on went to camps and house parties in different parts of the country to see new steam engines.

I went into the Army as my National Service and experienced God's keeping in tough situations with men whose background was very different from mine. This was followed by college to train as a teacher. That presented me with the different challenge of liberal theology, but the Christian Union saw me through that particular difficulty. I then taught in Gloucester and Leeds and became an elected leader of Roundhay Crusaders, later moving to Alwoodley and Headingly because of leadership needs. I left Crusader leadership when I left teaching and went into full-time youth work, but continued to do Westbrook Camps as Adjutant for seven years. In 1973 I was invited to become the leader of the Sportsman's Holiday, and that began twenty years of very special service with a wonderful team of officers. Towards the end we incorporated girls into the holiday and my wife, Sheila, and I had the privilege of being co-leaders on our last one in 1991.

My brother, Peter, went to university and became president of the Christian Union and later married Jean, the Lady Vice-President. They, together with their four children, served as missionaries at the Christian Medical College and Hospital at Vellore, Peter as an engineer. He then did an extra two years at St. Stephen's Hospital in Delhi.

On returning home for family reasons he served in various parts of the world as an engineer. At the age of seventy he was called back to Vellore to advise on new buildings.

I retired at the age of 58 to become the Secretary of the Readers of the Church of England at Church

House Westminster. Later, at the age of 68, I was ordained by the Archbishop of Canterbury to become Chaplain to the Elderly, working under Eric Delve, the international evangelist, at St, Luke's Church, Maidstone. Having worked with young people all my life, I now work with the elderly.

Humanly speaking I owe everything to Crusaders and to God's keeping power through sixty years. I wear a Crusader badge and old Crusaders recognise it and speak to me. They all have wonderful experiences to share and great respect for the Movement, and I encourage them along the way.

*   *   *

Gifts for Future Ministry

Rev Ian Hunter
Caterham / Sanderstead / Hartshorne Crusaders

I began Crusaders at Caterham in 1955 till approx 1958 before moving to Shirley for about 4 years. From there I went to Sanderstead. I left in 1972 to go to theological college.

Around 1996 I became involved with Crusaders again when we set up a group at the Church where I am Rector in Hartshorne.

The most important influence from Crusaders was that I was converted at a camp in Polzeath in Cornwall in 1957. This has influenced and affected my whole life and ministry.

Crusaders is therefore key to my becoming a Christian and therefore to my ministry to God in the Anglican Church over the past 32 years. I valued all the excellent teaching and grounding that I received in all the groups of which I was part. As I grew older Crusaders helped me to begin to exercise and realise the potential of the gifts God had given me for future ministry.

Taking the Gospel out

Herb Hackett

Merlswood / Snarebrook / Moor Park Crusaders

Just a note about my very happy involvement with Cru's some years ago – well, three quarters of a century ago actually!

Joining Merlswood and then Snaresbrook in the late 20s of the last century, I moved to Northwood in the 30s. There I reached the point of commitment at Ottershaw Easter House party in 1936 and became a leader at Moor Park Cru's (an offshoot from Northwood) where we met in my parents' house in fateful 1939.

During the war I was busy on various Fleet Air Arm Stations around the country and at each started a Young People's Bible Class linked with the local church. We catered for the local village children in each case but, sadly, they could not be linked with Cru's (In those days Cru's catered only for Public and Private school children). As a happy alternative I discovered the Covenanter Union – just like Crusaders except that the only restriction was that each group had to be attached to a church.

Over the years I enjoyed over 50 Covenanter Camps and Easter Broads Cruises and becoming Development Secretary and later Director of the movement. But, of course, I would rather have been involved with the Cru's to which, under God, I owe so much.

*   *   *

A Quiet Time Habit

John Abbiss, Dudley Crusaders

My association with Crusaders began in 1949, when, as a boy of fourteen, I was introduced to Dudley Class by my friends. Up until that point I was a regular member of the Bible Class at my local Anglican Church (where I still worship), but classes had been suspended at the start of an interregnum and the move to Crusaders was encouraged by my parents. I was made to feel 'at home' straight away by the Leaders (one of whom died recently – John Quayle) and was soon joining-in the many and varied activities so enjoyed by youngsters. Inter-class football and cricket matches were always favourites and the weekly Games Evenings, with an occasional 'wide game' in the country, were well attended. "Keenites" was also a regular commitment, usually held at a Leader's house, when we had the opportunity of praying together and studying the Bible.

It wasn't long before I sampled my first Cru Camp and linking with other boys from the Midlands classes, travelled by train to Studland. I couldn't believe how well-organised camp life could be and how much fun. It was at St David's camp the following year that I realised what being a Christian meant and decided that I would like to join that happy band. My Bible study continued in earnest after that and with the help of the Scripture Union Bible reading notes made my 'Quiet Time' an evening habit.

Back in the Sunday afternoon Cru Class I began playing the piano regularly for hymns (Golden Bells) and Choruses (CSSM) and this became the major part of my witness.

Two years National Service in the RAF temporarily broke my direct connection with the Dudley Class, but correspondence during that time from the Leaders was always encouraging. I was 'confirmed' during this time at a church in Salisbury and still have my little card signed by the Station Chaplain. When the Queen 'released me from duty' I soon renewed my link with Dudley and after a few years as an Assistant Leader, was honoured with an invitation to become a Leader. I was fortunate in Dudley Class to have some wonderful people to work with. We were a healthy mixture of denominations – Anglican, Methodist and Baptist – a blend that produced an efficient team with mutual respect.

The major change in Cru Class occurred when girls were invited to join us and ladies were pressed into augmenting our Leadership. I was thrilled to introduce my own two daughters to Crusaders and it has been very rewarding to see many of these girls (and boys too of course) mature into Christians with a strong faith. Dudley has a reputation for producing its own leaders and the source of committed people never seems to dry-up. With a strong new team at the helm, I felt it appropriate to resign from Leadership in 1995. It has given me the opportunity to take-on more responsibility at my church, but I shall always think of myself as a Crusader and, as an Honorary Life Member, still wear my badge with pride.

* * *

360 Degree About Turn

John Coatman, Croydon Crusaders

I was 8 years old when in 1949 my brother took me to Croydon Crusaders. It was something to do on a Sunday afternoon and I enjoyed the occasional parties and outings; the Sunday meetings were something to do on a weekend. Church was boring and Sunday suits!

I did not want to go to camp as to spend a week praying sounded boring. Christians were boring. I was invited to the Camps Rally in 1956 and was amazed to see people having fun at camp. I decided to give it a go but realised that I wasn't a Christian and so I set off to Studland that summer having made sure I was in the 'right group' by praying the 'little prayer' our leaders encouraged us to say. God had other ideas, and at camp that year He zapped me – I have never been the same again! Firstly, He changed my heart. I hated my old life and wanted to live for Him. He changed my voice. Out went dirty jokes and within days I was telling friends about Jesus. He changed my mind, having been in the bottom class at school I went to the top one, going on to university study for 9 years gaining a total of 5 both arts and science degrees. I ended up in teaching and gained an MA at the London Institute of Education and was a head teacher for 19 years.

All this time I remained in leadership of Croydon Crusaders. And then God pushed me to work for Crusaders and things reached their peak when I was appointed General Director. (The hardest job I have ever done!) Sadly, when 3 years ended at Head Office, I could only carry on in a voluntary basis but I have now completed over 57 years in Croydon Crusaders, 50 of them in leadership, and 9 years working full time for Crusaders.

My prayer when I became a Christian was that I should find another Christian at school. On the first day in assembly I looked at the boy next to me who I had never seen before and he was wearing a Crusader badge. My first answered prayer! We started a Christian Union which is still running and set about seeking to bring our fellow pupils to Christ. Very soon my leaders started trusting me with running activities for our group as my passion was that it should be fun.

I was only 22 when I ran my first house party for local groups and that passion for residential work has remained with my being away with young people about 12 times a year apart from many day trips. I have been involved in numerous ski trips and it was on one of these I had a serious fall: 100 metres down a mountain side hitting rocks as I went. I knew I was going to die and committed my soul to the Lord but I heard Him say 'No, I have still got work for you to do.' That was the third time in my life that I was spared. During the Second World War a 1000 pound bomb failed to explode outside our house. About a year later a German aircraft flew low over my mother and me shooting at us but missed by about 2 yards. I have a deep sense that God saved my life for me to serve Him. I hope to do so until my last day on earth.

*   *   *

An On-Going Pilgrimage

Dr Philip J Duke
Bridlington Crusaders / Moseley and Harbourne Crusaders

I can't remember when it was that one of my friends took me to the Crusader Class in Bridlington, East Yorkshire. It may have been in 1944 when I was around 12 years old. I didn't know it then but it was the start of an on-going pilgrimage. Our leader was Mr Priestman who lived near Hull in North Ferriby. From that distant point he took a keen interest in the class, but he left the running of the class in the more-than-capable hands of Mr R Turner, a flourishing florist in Bridlington. It was from him that I received my first clear Bible teaching and was encouraged to read the Scripture daily with the aid of Scripture Union notes. It was through him that I understood what it meant to be a Christian and to give my life to Jesus Christ. Later on I joined the Wednesday evening Bible class and absorbed more and more sound doctrine.

But Crusaders was not all Bible, though the Bible provided the foundation for all the class activities. There were the Saturday nights at 6.30pm. There were memorable evenings when I played chess with Mr Turner who was so absorbed in our game that almost anything could happen elsewhere... After a while these games were forbidden so that order could be maintained.

Bank Holiday specials were excursions to Ulrome, about 10 miles down the coast, where Mr Priestman had a cottage on the cliff top. We were often joined there by the girl Crusader class, a fascinating exposure to those mysterious beings from another world. (This was the 1940's!)

Soon my life with Crusaders expanded even further as the camps started after the war. My first was to St Bees in Cumberland – preceded by a wonderful train journey – with excursions to Wastwater and Great Gable. Soon I was going further afield – to Scotland. Blair Atholl, Aviemore, Ballater and other places are full of wonderful memories.

Crusaders not only gave me a precious grounding in the Christian faith but also introduced me to Christian service and the exercise of Christian leadership. I continued in active service with Crusaders in Birmingham (Moseley, with Dick Trew, and Harbourne) and later in Bristol under the inspiring leadership of Eddie LeRoy.

In 1959 I ceased to be involved with Crusaders when I moved to Abingdon and my work as a Lay Preacher in the Methodist Church took over. But it was Crusaders that prepared me for this ministry.

*   *   *

'Take the S.U. Next Sunday Please!'

Neil Johns
Ashford (Middlesex) Crusaders

I became a member of Ashford (Middx) Crusaders in 1940. My mother "arranged" for me to join the Class as I had become dissatisfied with Sunday Schools. [No reflection on them – I was the problem!]

What really impressed me, as a boy, was how smart the leaders looked! They all seemed very tall, they were cheerful, friendly and intelligent – and took us seriously. As a group they made an impression upon me.

The leader of Ashford Crusaders was a Mr George Lane, a civil servant, Brethren background – full of authority and yet a kindly man. Besides Crusaders, he and his wife (who looked rather like Queen Mary of the 1930's) ran a weeknight youth club and during the summer a Holiday Bible Club.

The leaders of the class expected each boy to become a Christian, and Mr Lane, during the class notices – about keenites, podex, etc. – would also include the name of any boy who had given his heart to the Lord. When I think back on those days, the level of Biblical teaching that we received was of the highest order. Later, when I became an assistant and full leader, I used George Goodman's handbook for Bible Study and in his advice to leaders, he writes, concerning preparation "take any amount of trouble" and that was what the leaders that taught me – in the Inters and Seniors – surely did!

We had lots of fun; the class was enjoyable. We wanted to be there. Activities included podex and wide games: We always drew a crowd of onlookers at podex because the game was a complete mystery outside of Crusaders. We had regular outings, including visits to London Zoo, when on one occasion, one boy decided to go home by himself! Mr Lane was very cross!

During the war (WW.2) we had some daylight air raids and our premises included a large basement where we all descended when the sirens went. One of my memories is of the Juniors sitting in a circle with their leader Frank Goldsmith balancing a Bible on one knee, and a Matthew Henry commentary on the other, while telling the Juniors to "be quiet" – during an air raid!

Like other classes, no doubt, an Inter or Senior was asked each Sunday to read and, if possible comment upon the Scripture Union portion for that Sunday. I later became involved in preaching and teaching Scripture, but my basic training was on being asked to "take the S.U. next Sunday, please" by one of the leaders.

As a Christian I owe a tremendous amount to Crusaders, and it was one Sunday afternoon, walking home from the class, that I asked the Lord Jesus to be my Saviour. Crusaders was of the Lord.

The Case for Ordination

Rev Peter Coombs Reading Crusaders

"A History of the World in 100 Objects" was one of last year's most interesting radio programmes. Its thesis was that 'Objects' speak for themselves and that through them people's lives stand revealed. My 'Object' would have to be a copy of the King James Version of the Bible. It is dog-eared, the spine is missing and the back cover is detached. Not surprising, perhaps after nearly seventy years of continuous use. The inscription on the fly leaf tells its own story:

READING CRUSADER CLASS

Presented to:

P B COOMBS

for regular attendance, July 1942

We are talking about 52 consecutive Sundays before the prized volume was placed in my hands with the singing of the SU Chorus No. 118

Make the Book live to me, O Lord
Show me Thyself within Thy Word
Show me myself and show me my Saviour
And make the Book live to me.

At the presentation – as the fly leaf reveals – I was given a text: Proverbs 8:17 'I love them that love me; and those that seek me early shall find me'. Within my Bible I carefully underlined that verse in ink. But not only that verse. Down the years many others were given the 'pen and ruler' treatment – verses that were special for me. My 'Object' is beginning to speak for itself.

But not only the Scriptures; the lives of the Class leaders also spoke powerfully. A.H. Brown, a physiotherapist and blinded in the Great War, Edgar Milward, leading Reading businessman and medicos Gledhill and Martin-Doyle.. Down to earth men of faith; what they were – quite as much as what they said – spoke volumes and they pointed to a Saviour utterly unique and always available to those who chose to follow Him.

Over the years the Crusader class and the Union gave me opportunity to exercise leadership myself. Camps and House parties at Westbrook, Bembridge and St. Davids all reinforced a growing conviction that I should offer for ordination. Looking back in 2011, I reckon that fifty years within the ministry of the Church of England began when a timid and not very articulate sixteen year old was given the opportunity to read and comment on the Scripture Union passage one Sunday at class.

This year, the 400th Anniversary of the King James Version of the Bible, many well-known figures are extolling the KJV as an essential part of our English heritage. Fine, but the Bible is so much more than that. It was the overriding 'Object' which defined my personal story. Through the written word, I discovered the living Word. How glad I am that P B Coombs (aged thirteen and a half) put in those twelve months of regular attendance. Had he not done so, where would he be now, I wonder?

Preparation for Ministry

Rev John M.F. Butler , Petersfield Crusaders

It was 4 September 1939: The day before I had sat with my parents listening to the sombre voice of Neville Chamberlain telling us that we were at war with Germany. Now I sat with some of my primary school contemporaries, but with well scrubbed knees, blue blazers proudly bearing the Churcher's College crest and our shiny new satchels – 'new bugs' beginning a fresh chapter in our education. Across the school hall sat another lot of boys, with different blazers and badges. They were the Emmanual School, from Wandsworth, evacuees come to Petersfield in Hampshire to share our homes, our classrooms and playing fields.

And with them came Greg Rodway, who was to be the vigorous leader of the Crusader Class they brought with them. Before long we settled happily into the rhythm of school life, with us having classes in the morning and games, OTC and cross country in the afternoon, they doing everything in reverse.

As soon as the Crusader Class got going, I went along, and in a while found myself standing nervously in front of the class to read the Scripture Union portion and stammer out the very few thoughts I had had about it. Outings to seaside and country, the occasional very special meal in a restaurant with Greg, Misty memories of Studland – white house, white bell tents, white sands – mark those years. Most memorable of all, towards the end of the war, a visit to Upper Tooting and Wandsworth Crusader Class to meet Robert Ewan their leader, and listen to the venerable Hudson Pope, a well known and much used children's evangelist from CSSM. 'Sin lieth at the door' he quoted in one of his talks, and in the back row I bowed my head and opened my heart to the One who could save from sin and give new life.

The war ended and Emmanual School went home. But we continued the Class, and I became for a while, a leader. A weekend at Hoddesdon, among dozens of other leaders and trainee leaders was very special. I left school at 16, after an undistinguished five years, to become a Post Office Engineer, and thereafter to do my National Service. In 1949, I entered New College, London to prepare for the ministry.

Greg and I sent cards at Christmas, but met only once more, when I applied to become the General Secretary of Scripture Union in Scotland. Greg was sent by John Laird, the then English Secretary, to check me out. He must have given a good report, as I got the job, and spent the next twenty three years happily involved with an organisation that has always been closely allied with Crusaders.

A Life in Leadership

Ros Holt, Hove Crusaders

Following a house move further away from my family church, I was introduced to a local Crusader Class in Hove by some school friends when I was about 10 years old, over 50 years ago.

The Class squashed into the former nursery of a large family house. The room was reached by the back stairs each Sunday afternoon. The well-to-do lady of the house was a great servant of the Lord and eventually taught the older girls from her bed when ill. I loved the Bible teaching and especially the 'chorus' time. A Bible verse can still prompt the singing of a CSSM chorus learnt all those years ago! Singing the scriptures has been a part of my life ever since.

Regular attendance was rewarded with a Crusader badge after 10 consecutive weeks, a New Testament after a further 25 weeks, and a Crusader Bible, boxed and beautifully bound, after a further 50 weeks. Participation was always encouraged at Crusaders and I took my turn at reading the passage for the day and giving a little comment. This was a great training environment and I still have those little notes tucked in the front of my Crusader Bible. The older girls were good role models and the leaders mostly young and enthusiastic. Two school friends who were Crusaders have been great supports to me recently since I have been widowed.

In my teens I started to go to Easter house parties and it was at one of these when I was 14 that I responded personally to the gospel. Again, the commitment and the example of Christian love and living of the leaders impressed me. Activities and trips were organised, as well as morning and evening devotions and we all made new friends each time. I visited new parts of the country as far away as

Yorkshire and North Wales and finally went on a walking holiday round Snowdonia.

My first experiences of helping and then teaching a group of children were at Crusaders. When I moved away to college I helped at a newly launched local Crusader Class which my own daughter later joined.

The evangelical approach to the Scriptures that I encountered at Crusaders has been a mainstay of my life and I have led Sunday school classes, children's clubs, nurture groups, Bible study groups and spoken at ladies' meetings over the years. God has never called me to preach – that was my husband's calling – but I have been a worship leader for a number of years.

The Jesus I met through Crusaders is still Lord of my life, and He has never let me down. He enabled me to have that wonderful grounding in the faith through Crusaders and I am so very grateful.

*   *   *

From 'Timothy' to Church Youth Worker

Phil Pittard, Timothy / Area Development Worker (Kent)

Having been a voluntary leader in two Worthing groups I applied for and was taken on as a "Timothy" in Yorkshire working with Malcolm Loveday who was then the Area Development Worker (ADW) for that area. I spent a year taking part in school assemblies, assisting and taking sessions at various groups, preaching in church, taking part in Crusader holidays and many other varied and interesting tasks. It was a fantastic grounding which formed the foundation for taking on the post in 1992 of ADW for Kent.

I was probably the youngest ADW taken on at that stage and I joined a diverse and extremely talented team.

The staff meetings were a key feature of our role and an opportunity to meet up with other ADWs. These were times of fun, learning and support.

As part of my role I worked with Ian MacDonald at the recently renamed "Time Out" conference running the night entertainment. A special memory was of getting a fit of uncontrollable laughter while on stage as Ian interviewed Steve Chalke. Ian asked a question so long that everybody in the room lost his train of thought including Steve and Ian.

At a more local level I was part of the team which worked with John Eakins (Senior ADW) and Paul Rush (Sussex and Portsdown ADW) as they pioneered the Spree camps. I remember having over 1000 people on site and recognising that we had bitten off a little more than we could chew (apologies for all those I annoyed while using the louder speaker system, the power went rather to my head). I also enjoyed writing the outline for the 'Challenge of a Lifetime' Roadshow that toured the country and challenged many young people's lives.

I worked for Crusaders until 1997. I went on to work in a local church as a youth worker (Lancing Crusaders was based at the church) and finish my degree in Theology, which had been recommended to me as part of taking on the ADW role in Kent.

Probably the fondest memory I have of that time were the local volunteer leaders who gave up so much to support me in a whole variety of ways, a huge thank you to them!

*   *   *

ADW to Mentoring Training

Sharon Prior, Area Development Work (East Midlands)

 I first got involved with Crusaders in 1985 just before going off to Bible College. I went on an Enfield Crusader camp at St David's as a favour to a friend to cook for them. Following that year I never looked back!

After Bible College I became an Area Development Worker for Crusaders firstly in North London and then in the East Midlands. I enjoyed my five years working in this capacity and learnt a lot from the great people who I worked alongside. Two people who I remember most are Ernie Addicott and Heather Keep. Both of them taught me what it means to live a godly life and the importance of living a prayerful life. This is something I will never forget.

During this time I also got involved in leading camps at Studland and over the years I have met some great team members and young people on those holidays. These were times of great fun and lots of laughter whilst we learnt together about Jesus and his amazing love for us. The Leaders went on camps to teach the young people about Him, but I can honestly say that the young people taught be so much about faith and what it means to stand up for Jesus when it is really tough to do so. So there was very much a sense of mutual learning and sharing together.

Once you get involved in an organisation like Crusaders it is very hard to imagine what it was like before you got involved, because the people you meet become like family to you. Hence I am still involved 26 years later!

I first found my love for mentoring within the movement, as I saw the way that lives were transformed by having intentional relationships with team members and young people alike. These have been great opportunities to encourage, empower and challenge young people to be all that God has created them to be. During my time with Crusaders not only has my life been transformed, but I have witnessed many other lives turned around through the power of Jesus.

I was also part of the National Training Team and we spent many weekends travelling around the country training leaders to be even more effective in their work with young people. This was a real privilege and it was great to work alongside Brenda Cuthbert and Brain Spurling. The thing I was impressed with most on these training weekends was the number of volunteers who faithfully worked with young people week after week, sometimes in very difficult situations, but they provided a consistency for young people that might have been the only stable thing in their lives at that time. Some leaders worked in very small groups, but they didn't get discouraged they continued to do what God had called them to; what an amazing witness!

My time (which still continues) with Crusaders is one of making great friends, seeing God move powerfully in young people's lives and witnessing the dedication and faithfulness of the Crusader Leaders.

*   *   *

From Londonderry to Trustee

John Magowan, Trustee for Urban Saints

Little did I realise that when I accepted an invitation from a friend, with whom I have long since lost contact, to attend Londonderry Crusaders in November 1956, that it would lead to the organisation playing such a large part in my life and that now, fifty five years later, I would still be involved as a member of the Board of Trustees.

The Londonderry Class was led for the first fifty years of its eighty year old existence by TS Mooney, an archetypical bachelor who believed "in giving women the right hand of fellowship but keeping them at arm's length" and whose commitment to the boys in his care was total – his goal was to ensure that each had "a Book in his hand, a Saviour in his heart and a purpose in his life." An outstanding Bible teacher, Sunday by Sunday he taught us the great truths of Scripture in a very clear, interesting manner. I can still see him standing at the front of class, without one bit of the now requisite technology in sight, empowered by the Holy Spirit, bringing to life many Bible stories by means of his vivid use of the English language and apt use of illustration.

TS always encouraged us to take part in the various "Union Activities" so I attended the Easter house party at Bangor on the County Down coast in 1958 – my first holiday away from home without my family. There I met many boys from the other Classes in Ireland and made several lasting friendships. More importantly, the Lord used the Padre's talks that weekend to give me a real assurance of faith following the commitment I had made three months earlier.

That weekend cemented my relationship to Crusaders. I attended each Sunday throughout the rest of my schooldays benefitting, not only from the regular weekly fellowship, but also from a remarkably wide variety of activities organised by the dedicated leaders of the small group of twelve classes which formed the Union in Ireland in those days. Activities which included summer camps on the North Coast at Castlerock, the aforementioned house parties, the six-a-side soccer competition, the sports – both summer and winter, to name but a few.

On returning from university in 1967 to teach in my old school, TS was quick to enlist me into the leadership of the Class – a role I fulfilled for the next forty years. It has been a great privilege to serve in this way with so many other faithful leaders, to enjoy their fellowship and to see so many boys and girls (the Class became co-ed in the late eighties) come to faith and now hold positions of leadership, both Christian and secular, in various parts of the UK and beyond.

It was a joy to attend the eightieth Birthday Service in December 2010 and, amongst the greetings, to hear one from a remarkable 94 year old retired minister who attended the inaugural meeting of the Class in 1930! He was giving thanks to God for the work of Londonderry Crusaders. With countless others down the generations I gladly join him in that prayer.

Dyffryn 1969

CHAPTER FIVE

The Three 'F's

– Fellowship, Friendship and Fun

'On the third day a wedding took place in Cana in Galilee. Jesus' mother was there and Jesus and his disciples had also been invited to the wedding'.

John 2 v 1-2.

Crusaders has a reputation for building friendships and relationships. It's what would be termed 'relational youthwork' from which friendships are built and young people develop. Not just about the Spiritual side of Christianity, because for some that wasn't important, but the fun, fellowship and lifelong friendships that have been built up through many years. The social side of Crusaders deepened many people's desire to attend the regular Sunday meetings and thereby enabling the Spirit to work and God's People to take their place.

From the local groups came other Fellowships that met regularly giving the Seniors the opportunity to meet with like-minded people. This became an important fixture as it meant that girls and boys were able to enjoy fellowship together. The Wellesley Fellowship is one such group, other similar groups around the UK gave the same opportunities, cemented friendships which are still very much in evidence today.

We did the things boys love to do

Rev Graham Sinden, Godalming and Haslemere Crusaders

Setting off for Godalming Crusaders with brothers and friends, around 1965. Graham Sinden (fourth right) in between my two brothers.

Crack! Splinter! Another record broken – literally! Godalming Crusader Class was growing and every time the numbers increased, another 78 rpm vinyl record (this was the 1960s) scattered round the hall in bits.

Crusaders was such a change from dreary Sunday school. It was fun. We did things that boys love to do, like energetic games, messing about in boats and sports, and it was just for boys! Crusaders was an adventure. There were activities such as canoeing and abseiling and regular camps. One, at St David's in 1969, was nearly blown away when we were struck by a force 9 gale and were evacuated to a farmer's barn.

We had trips to places like the Portsmouth Dockyard and competitive games of football against the local Covenanters. Famous people came to visit. Olympic gold medallist David Hemery spoke at an anniversary and even Cliff Richard came.

On Sunday afternoons my brother Clive and I, plus two other friends, cycled from Farncombe two miles into Godalming to the Congregational hall, joined later by my brother David. Every Sunday we heard the Christian message presented in a way that was lively, intelligent and authentic. We sang choruses from the new *Youth Praise*. Our leaders were a great bunch, drawn from a spread of Christian traditions, Anglican, Baptist, Brethren. They put up with a lot, including being pegged out at camp! The younger leaders gave us boys an attractive model of what it meant to follow Christ.

For me, the Christian faith was a 'given'. My parents were Christians so I went along with it. Then when I was at a class camp in my young teens, I realised for the first time the need for me to actually do something with this message of Christ, but it was not until I was 17 at a joint camp in North Wales in 1971, that I responded. There were some older boys from another class talking about predestination. I had never heard of it, but that night I talked theology with my close friend Noel. It was theology that got personal for I realised in a way that I had never seen before that Christ had died for me. That night in my sleeping bag I surrendered my life to Jesus Christ.

About a year before this, the family moved ten miles to Hindhead. For a time, we were ferried to the Godalming class. This came to an end when a new class was started in Haslemere, much closer to home. We met at a new youth centre in the town and while the group was smaller than we were used to, the number of boys grew with more records smashed.

Two memories of this time stand out. Every year Crusaders held a national athletics day at Motspur Park. One year we won the cup for the highest achieving of the smaller classes. The other memory was my first attempt at preaching. Crusaders had been asked to take an evening service in Haslemere. I had been baptised in November 1972 and around that time had felt a call from God to enter the Christian ministry as a pastor. Following training, I became a Baptist minister and have served at three churches, currently at Kidlington Baptist in Oxfordshire.

In my late teens, God became real to me and turned my life around. It was through the work of Crusaders that the message became real through the faithful, patient, sacrificial witness of Crusader leaders and older boys. One of the songs we used to sing in those days summed up my desire at that time, 'For me to live is Christ, to die is gain'. I will always be grateful to God for this movement.

*   *   *

Wellesley Fellowship
– Heady Years of Socialising

Frances Marchant (nee Wright, married to Gordon Collin 1967-69), Carshalton Beeches Girl Crusaders 1947-1958 and Wellesley Fellowship from 1956

My memories of being a Girl Crusader from the late 1940s are many and varied. Being a "good" little girl, I obediently and willingly "gave my heart to Jesus" whenever invited to do so (most weeks, I seem to remember).

The annual texts went up on my bedroom wall when they came through. The one that I particularly warmed to was "I will never leave thee nor forsake thee" (Hebrews 13 v 5) which I've never forgotten.

The leaders of the Class were inspirational. Dot Guyatt held a group of 7-year-olds spellbound with a visual aid of a garden illustrating the parable of the sower. Lucy Smart (who died aged 90) took, what seemed like an interminable series on Pilgrims Progress with a class of fidgety teenage girls, and another on Revelation – "Is your name written in the Lamb's Book of Life?" But they cared about us and used to give us time away from the usual Class meetings. We used to travel with other teenagers in the back of Lucy's mini-traveller, all of us somewhat alarmed by her habit while driving of turning her head an apparent 180 degrees to talk to those of us in the back seat.

At the age of 18, I was invited to become an Assistant Leader, which I turned down. Why? Because it would have meant not being allowed to wear make-up or going to the cinema.

The Girl Crusader Union's teaching on sex in those days was very simple – "girls are different from boys", and therefore of course shouldn't mix. Fortunately Randle Manwaring (of Sutton Boys and Wellesley Fellowship) thought differently, and we enjoyed the heady years of socialising with all the local classes of both sexes from the ages of 16 upwards, including annual house parties, monthly meetings, Bible studies, musical evenings, tennis …. making friendships which have lasted over 50 years and consolidating faith which will last through eternity. Here I met my first husband, Gordon Collin (Randle was a good matchmaker!) and later was prayed for and supported by the members of the Wellesley Fellowship through bereavement at Gordon's early death.

Many years later, whilst running holiday cottages with my second husband in Wales, we had the joy of hosting a local Crusader class Saturday Swims in our swimming pool, and also a Junior Alpha – and experienced the joy of witnessing a baptism in the pool.

What was the most important thing I learnt during my time with Crusaders? I learnt that Jesus loves me and died for me, I learnt to read, know and trust the Bible as the Word of God – and I learnt (probably almost more importantly!) that God loves ALL those who respond to his love and invitation, and is no respecter of denominational differences!

We throw chairs

Rev Joe Ridholls, Plymouth Crusaders

My Sunday School teacher was what you might call a saint. She had to be to put up with me! Saint or no saint, I was bored through no fault of hers. I suspect I would soon have been an ex-Sunday School Scholar. But then, one day at school, one of my mates approached me, "Joe, you ought to come to Crusaders". They met at Mutley Baptist Church, Plymouth on Sunday afternoons. Immediately I was suspicious. "It's not a Sunday School, is it?" I asked, "What do you do?" He was adamant it was not a Sunday School and went on enthusiastically to explain what Crusaders did. "We go out in boats! We go for hikes on the Moors and on Sunday afternoons we have fights and throw chairs at one another!" Great! Just what I had been looking for! I nagged my Mother who eventually and, with great reluctance, let me leave Sunday School and go to Crusaders. I discovered that my enthusiastic friend had been somewhat economical with the truth. True we went out in boats and we went for hikes on the Moors (which left me with a lifelong love of Dartmoor) but on no Sunday afternoon did I have a fight or throw, or be hit by, a chair!

He had been part of a recruiting campaign for this Evangelical Boys' Bible Class. How many times have I thanked God for him, for I really came to enjoy Crusaders and received Christ as my Saviour and Lord during as Easter Campaign led by the redoubtable John Laing, founder of the internationally-known Laing Builders and Engineers and a devout Christian man. We sang gutsy choruses (*Marching beneath the banner, fighting beneath the Cross*), we listened to punchy, relevant Biblical messages and enjoyed being with our mates from school. We went camping, enjoyed sport, had fun, and all in the company of real, down-to-earth Christian men. Ernest Uren and Norman Sitters were leaders at that time. From an intake of just a few years, some dozen or so boys became full-time clergy; two of them, Don Snelgrove and Ken Pillar, becoming Bishops! Plymouth church life owes much to the Crusader movement but I also recall the Sarsons from the Torquay area and now there are Crusader Groups in Cornwall. Groups in St Dennis and Perranporth and one still thriving in the Roseland area - which I started!

In summing up what Crusaders is all about, I quote the Crusader chorus: '

> *The Lord hath need of me,*
> *His soldier I will be.*
> *He gave Himself my life to win*
> *and so I mean to follow Him*
> *and serve Him faithfully.*
> *And, although the fight be fierce and long,*
> *I'll carry on He makes me strong.*
> *And then, one day, His face I'll see and,*
> *Oh the joy when He says to me*
> *"Well done, my brave Crusader!"'*

*   *   *

The Irish Brothers who needed Scottish Crusaders!

Maurice D.S. Farquhar, Corstophine Crusaders

It was in 1969 that my brother George and I began attending the Crusaders in Corstorphine, West Edinburgh. As a family in Christian activities already – our parents worked with The Faith Mission – we had moved from Northern Ireland. A good friend had told us of Crusaders, which was a mere 15 minutes' cycle from home! The founder of the group, Dr Andrew Boyd, was still involved but the group was ably led by 'the three wise men': Ken Robertson, Alan Walker and Ian Spence.

It's no exaggeration to say that these faithful, sincere, godly men had an immensely positive influence on our young lives for at least 21 significant years; years when we passed from 'being boys' to the challenges of becoming adults. I pay special tribute to Ken, Alan and Ian as I remember with gratitude to God their entire patient teaching, time and dedication every Sunday afternoon. I recall great fun in our Bible Quiz; plenty of musical originality from Alan at the piano, and serious yet practical discussions with other young folk. George and I will be forever grateful for having this precious opportunity to absorb God's word together in an open and upbeat atmosphere. Space does not permit details of events like annual Birthday services, or the swimming gala at the Commonwealth Pool, those tremendous weekends away in beautiful scenery or fellowship with our peers as we took our turn as assistant leaders. The joy, however, of being part of a team and part of the wider Crusader movement was very real. If we had not been blessed with Crusaders – and Corstorphine Crusaders in particular – our lives would certainly have been poorer.

The 1990s brought many changes. The Corstorphine group closed, although another one nearby was started. The leadership team moved on to other commitments both professionally and spiritually, but several friendships remained important to us. What a gift to have good Christian friends who can support us and pray with us in times of loss, celebration or change! By 2001, God had led us both through various circumstances back to live in Northern Ireland once again.

Now, in 2006, George is a Ward Clerk in Belfast City Hospital. He is a church elder, enjoys choral singing and is involved with other Christian work. I enjoy supporting my wife Gabrielle, minister in Ballycarry Presbyterian Church, County Antrim. I give piano lessons, and facilitate people with disabilities to make music using specialised computer technology. I also teach a Bible Class and assist with Faith Mission summer camps for teens. A varied life indeed!

May the Lord enable us all to keep 'looking unto Jesus' especially in today's amazing and needy society. Thank you, Crusaders for continuing the work as 'Urban Saints'.

*   *   *

Lifelong Friendships

Grace Neal, Ampleforth Crusaders

I attended my first Crusader meeting, aged 10 in January 1999, not knowing anybody else there. I returned home that Friday evening feeling really empowered and moved by Crusaders, and what it does. I've used that same energy over the past seven years to attend meetings, make new friends, bring some old ones to the group, and complete my Infusion course.

Crusaders has given me so much in spiritual and social terms, I'll be forever working hard for them, for the glory of God in return. My *Infusion* course brought my faith to the forefront of my life, which has remained there ever since. The fantastic leaders have helped me discover who I am as a Christian, as well giving me new and exciting ways to worship God, and tell others His Good News. Everything I get involved with within Crusaders is deeply moving, witnessing how God has changed, and is changing so many lives. The leaders are dedicated to following Christ and their dependence of prayer still amazes me.

I have made many lifelong friends through Crusaders, who offer me support and new opportunities constantly. Hearing Matt Summerfield speak about how brilliant God is, is like a shot in the heart, a sudden reminder of how privileged I am to have a relationship with the Lord, and how I should sustain this so others can have one with Him too. From attending my first meeting of 10 Crusaders crammed into a small cottage, to my first Council Meeting at Head Office which really opened my eyes to the 'bigger picture' of Crusaders, and what they're doing on a national and international scale. Now I'm feeling that sudden burst of excitement all over again for the 10 year olds who go to their first meetings…

A Team Player

Rachel Haigh (nee Nunnerley), Redditch Crusaders

My brother and I were the only children in our church so we did not have a Sunday School or interaction with other Christian young people. When I was eighteen I joined St Peter's C of E in Redditch and made some Christian friends there which was great. One of the young married men brought the Crusaders to Redditch and invited several of our church group to join with him in this work. It soon became very apparent to me that I had missed out so much in my restricted young Christian experience. It opened a new world to me and broadened my horizons giving me experience of working in a team which has stood me in good stead as a missionary in Africa... My widowed mother loved it when some of these young Crusaders came home with me for tea.

I married a missionary serving in Zambia and in 1977 went there with him to share in that work. We lived in a remote area of Zambia, over 300 miles from the nearest town on the borders of Angola and Zaire. The Lord gave us two sons, Ivan and Peter, who were brought up and did all of their education in Zambia. I really wanted the boys to experience something of life in UK so we decided to send them to a Crusader camp in Keswick. This gave them experiences they had never had in Africa and they made many new young friends.

They attended another camp on the Isle of Wight during Ivan's first year of university. Here he was smitten by one of the beautiful leaders called Fiona whom he has since married. They have since acted as leaders at several of these camps on the Isle of Wight.

I am very grateful to the Lord for those days with Crusaders and the friends made then who have taken an interest in our lives as missionaries.

The Highlight was Railway Night

John Talbot. Finchley, Banstead, Wellesley Fellowship and Grimsby Crusaders

It was 1937/8 Crusaders came into my life through Finchley Juniors, graduating through Inters and Seniors until the family moved to Surrey.

The highlight of any week in Finchley was the Thursday evening 'Railway Night' at the home of Mr & Mrs Herbert Bevington. Herbert had glass fronted bookcases full of gauge 'O' (clockwork) locomotives, with lots of carriages kept in the garden shed terminus. The railway ran the length of the garden with cries of '*Out Waterloo*'; or '*In Victoria*' at one end and 'out Brockenhurst' at the other.

Following the Talbot family move to Surrey I was introduced to Leatherhead Crusaders with Francis Coningsby when home on leave from the Merchant Navy. On coming ashore and taking a job in London, I became an Assistant Leader with Banstead (boys) Crusaders. In addition to a few joint activities with the local Girls Crusader Group (of course arrangements were always deputed to the unmarried leaders from each group). The annual Banstead Boys Easter house parties at Westbrook required the provision of cooks. Well done to the Girl Crusaders again – under the guidance of Heather and Hilary Wood, Doreen Street and (ultimately to become my wife) Lesley Sharman – I had to make sure she could cook at least for 60 people, so I assumed cooking for 2 would be no problem! The cooks not only enjoyed themselves at Westbrook, but enjoyed continued informal gatherings in Surrey with the other young leaders at Martin Blossom's static caravan which was parked near the top of Reigate Hill.

Banstead Crusaders also introduced me to the wonders of the local monthly Wellesley Fellowship gatherings for Leaders and 16+ Seniors from all the local groups in the Sutton area. Many hilarious and enjoyable annual weekend house parties took place, with the establishment of the Bachelors Club of which yours truly became Secretary, until forced to resign from that position, on becoming engaged to Banstead Assistant Leader (girls) Crusaders Lesley Sharman and our subsequent marriage in 1964. It was many years later that David Rivett (Bachelors Club Chairman) succumbed to the charms of Sally (née Duncan). Wellesley Fellowship provided many good friendships over the years.

From Surrey we moved to Grimsby via London and Hertfordshire, eventually being part of a group of ex Crusaders who brought Grimsby Crusaders into being. The coming together was very much "Right for the Time". Our own family grew up within that group, making friends and enjoying the teaching from a range of dedicated Christians over many years, together with involvement in Regional Crusader activities of which the Yorkshire Swimming Galas – held in Wetherby, Doncaster and then Chappletown (Sheffield) became one of the highlights. However, the group closed in 1994 after nearly twenty years, but has re-started in more recent years under new leaders.

A Great Social Life

Barbara Nunn, Sidcup Crusaders

Yes, it was many years ago that I determined to go to Crusaders. It was my fifteenth birthday and my parents had eventually allowed me to make contact with the Sidcup class, which had Mrs Downes, or much loved 'Downie', as leader.

I joined the Seniors' class who were studying the long words of our faith, such as regeneration, justification and sanctification – 'tough stuff' for a fifteen year old, but it was in the Lord's timing and within a couple of weeks I had realised that I was not regenerate. Although not at all sure what my sins were, I prayed for forgiveness and gave my young life to Jesus, and He has truly blessed me with 'life abundant', as I have journeyed through the various stages of my life.

I enjoyed fellowship with the other girls, especially as most of them came from Christian homes: we played tennis together every Tuesday evening, at the home of one of the girls, and met in another home on Sunday evenings for a Bible quiz, giving me my life-long love of God's word; on Bank Holiday weekends, we would meet for a ramble with some of the Boys' class, including Robert Hunt, later Chairman of Crusaders. One year, five of us girls had a super cycling holiday together, through the Kent and Surrey countryside.

Quite naturally, relationships formed and a precious first memory of my future husband was his kneeling at a chair, praying, in the lounge of our Crusader leaders' home. The war drew several of us into the Services, but we kept in touch; a sheaf of letters was circulated, to this you added a fresh letter, and withdrew your last one. I realised how blessed I was, with so many Crusader friends.

Post war, we seemed to keep in touch year by year, with the many weddings, to which we were all invited, of course! But sadly in 1980, it was a funeral, my husband's funeral, and regret was expressed that we had met only for a sad occasion. So plans were made to meet annually, on the second Tuesday of each May, and the nucleus of the group was the same as that for tennis, in pre war days, (with four or five spouses added). That one day of the year became a very special day: for many it meant travelling from far and wide, to meet at the host's home, with the need to book into a B & B for a couple of nights. We took turns to host the day, providing morning coffee, lunch, a light tea after a walk, boat trip, or something local – concluding with a hot evening meal – over the years it was simplified somewhat!

After meeting in this way for twenty five years, some members were unable to cope with the long day, and the long distance to be travelled, so sadly 'our day' was brought to a close, but leaving a life time of Crusader memories.

*   *   *

Life With Meaning

Doreen Street, Wellesley Fellowship, Cheam, Worcester Park and Sutton Crusaders

I started at Cruettes (Mini-Crus) at the age of 4 at a house near our home in New Malden. When I was 6, I went on to a proper Crusader Group in another home and went on to

make many friends there. There were, of course, outings and teas and it was all fun as well as at Sunday classes. I still remember some of the talks even now! I then transferred to Cheam when the New Malden leader moved and ultimately became a Leader there for several years. After that I helped to start the Worcester Park Group and finished my Leadership at Sutton. Always there were numerous games evenings and outings, sometimes with other local Groups.

It was a joy to me to work at Crusader H.Q. at Ludgate Hill for Jack Watford, and consequently met many Leaders from all over the country. I cooked at Studland and Westbrook camps and also helped at the Swiss house parties over the years.

Our area around Sutton had many Cru Classes and it was wonderful as Seniors to be able to join the Wellesley Fellowship, which was formed for the older Seniors and past members. Main meetings were once a month with a renowned speaker, but there were monthly Bible studies, musical evenings, socials and outings, all of which grounded us in Life with meaning.

Crusaders has always been part of my life, and a very important part. When Graham and I married, he had joined Sutton Crusaders as a Senior incomer and later became a Leader at Stoneleigh & Cheam, where our sons ultimately joined. The teaching, on what was always Sunday, was a wonderful grounding which I hope we were able to pass on to others. Since "retirement" we have met many ex-Crusaders now in full-time ministry, and all have had praise for the teaching at Crusaders.

*   *   *

We Loved the Fun of Crusader Activities

Douglas Austin, Erdington and Leamington Crusaders

It all began, so far as I can remember, one Saturday afternoon in May 1939. I was ten years old and a junior member of Bishop Vesey's Grammar School, Sutton Coldfield. My parents and I were attending the school annual athletics sports day. I sat enthralled as my boyhood hero won the open mile. Alan Jewels was not only an outstanding sportsman, he was also a Crusader! Sitting next to my parents was Noel Crocker, a joint leader with John Miles, and Sam Burns of the Birmingham / Erdington Crusader class. My parents were impressed by what they heard about 'Crusaders' and following Noel's invitation, it was not long afterwards that I became a member of the Erdington class.

I loved going to the class. I was inspired by the leaders who were right on my wavelength; it was not long before I earned my Crusader badge as a result of attending ten consecutive Sundays.

In August 1941, I went along with my friends Hector Mackenzie and Philip Woods to my first Crusader house party. It was there that I heard the gospel so clearly presented by a head master called Gordon Humphreys and by 'Bubbly' Head that I responded positively to its message. As I write these words, I have before me the New Testament from those days with the words I wrote on the front cover inside page:

'I was converted on Sunday August 31st 1941 at Bilton Grange Crusader house party'

Coming home, my friends and I found such joy in meeting every Wednesday evening at 'Keynites' where we were firmly grounded in the Scriptures. We loved the fun and sheer delight in joining in Crusader activities. We played hockey in Sutton Park, and Podex and Crocker whenever we could! We enjoyed each other's company at special events put on by leaders at regional and national levels.

We also went to camps together with our friends and found ourselves tent officers at age fifteen as older teenagers were away fighting Hitler!

At sixteen we were encouraged to join the local Crusader fellowship which meant we could meet with girls from the girls Crusader class! Yippee! It was here that I met Joy Jones, who, later, in 1953, became my wife for fifty-four glorious years, until her home call in 2007. We were truly blessed with three wonderful children, Elizabeth, Heather and Andrew.

In 1954 we moved to Leamington Spa where I had the privilege of becoming a joint leader with Jack Oliver and Phil Rodway. In this Leamington Crusader class we were later joined in leadership by Peter Carroll and Peter Searle.

What a debt I owe to Crusaders. I learnt early on that Jesus is Lord and that in all things He should have pre-eminence, and that the ultimate purpose of life is to become like Him and make Him known to others.

*   *   *

A Friendship to Last a Lifetime

Glyn Macaulay, Birkenhead Crusaders

 As I jot down my reminiscences I am sitting with two other dinosaurs of Crusaders, Bill Latham and Graham Disbrey, both editors of the Magazine in their time. In my younger days I was based in Birkenhead and Bill and Graham in Finchley, both great Crusader classes in those days of the 1950's. Our friendship came via camps, particularly Polzeath, and has survived over fifty years. That's one of my outstanding memories of Crusaders – friendships.

Birkenhead was a bustling, thriving group in those days led by Sydney Proctor and Will Rankin. We arrived at about 2.45pm on Sunday afternoon, dressed in school blazers and ties and recited the previous week's memory verse which together with bringing a Bible earned valuable points for our team. Even more points were obtained by bringing a new recruit and an additional bonus if the recruit earned his badge by doing 10 consecutive Sundays. Boys, and of course it was only boys, had to attend a grammar school on an approved list to join the Class.

We were excited each Sunday when the "returns" for the previous week were read out. These told us how our attendance compared with other groups. We were very competitive! I look back in gratitude at the way we were encouraged to participate on Sunday afternoons, introducing the choruses and commenting on the Scripture reading, a great training for Christian leadership in the future.

The annual "birthday" and "union" Sundays were highlights of our year and on one memorable occasion, we welcomed Lt. Gen. Sir Arthur Smith, the President of

Crusaders, as our guest speaker. Everything was organised in great detail as folklore had it that one class badly overran the service timetable and it was after 4pm when Sir Arthur was asked to give his address. "Sander" (Sandhurst) he replied, and sat down telling a very embarrassed leader that "they had had enough already".

Then there was Westbrook, the Union's new (in 1948) War Memorial property on the Isle of Wight. For an 11 year old Birkolian to have the opportunity to travel to London, go across the capital and then down to Portsmouth and on the boat to the island was an enormous project. When I was a few years older, I moved on to the New Year Westbrook House Party and this has outstanding memories. During the week, we walked down to Ryde, late at night, trying to avoid the breakers as they hit the sea wall. One year with the holiday over-subscribed, some of us slept in the games hut and became the "outhouse men". "Two, four, six, eight, ten, here we come the…" Also what a thrill to stay on at the end of one holiday to help Mr. and Mrs Vereker on a work party.

Then there are the Polzeath memories: I so vividly recall Kenneth Anderson, a senior city engineer, playing "hunt the officer" and lying covered in tomato ketchup on a cliff top path. Unfortunately, before the campers were let loose, an elderly couple, out for an afternoon stroll, found Kenneth. When he told them to go away, as they were spoiling a game, he was given a severe dressing down, and retired from the game before it started. Kenneth will always be remembered for playing his battered old squeeze-box at evening prayers.

My major recollection is of outstanding Christian leadership and this constantly challenged me in later years when I realised the responsibility I had. I could never imagine the lads in my group benefiting from my life and teaching as I had enjoyed as a youngster. It was a great privilege a couple of years ago to visit Will Rankin then in his mid nineties in a Nursing Home and personally thank and pray with him.

CHAPTER SIX

Camps, House Parties and Overseas!

'I press on towards the goal to win the prize for which God has called me heavenwards in Christ Jesus.'

Philippians 3 v 14

What was it that made Crusader camping so unique and so enjoyable an experience? The basic ingredient was and remains, a group of officers dedicated to Christ and concerned to serve Him in serving the youngsters under their care. Until the late 90s the holiday programme would all start with a day conference in London which brought the holiday leaders and their teams together to meet and pray and plan for their holiday. It was a great day to meet new friends, greet old friends and get excited as to what the Lord was going to do, as well as allocate duties. In earlier days there was a military feel to the camp and staff officers were known as 'Commy', 'Adjy', 'Quarters' and 'Subby'. In later times these were dropped and the main roles included Leaders (Senior, Junior and Overall), Chaplain, Organiser and Caterer.

Activities on camps have rarely altered in essence. Early morning swims, room or tent inspection, wide games including the Crusader favourites of 'crocker', 'hacker' and 'podex', Hunt the Officer in local towns or seaside promenades bring chaos and embarrassment on occasion, the statutory day out and in-house tournaments of table tennis and the obligatory swimming gala.

Main parties ran from London both outward and back where a whole carriage would be taken up by this group of noisy, excited young people, making friends, sharing experiences. I remember standing on the platform at Doncaster Station waiting for my train to arrive and as it approached dad being very excited that it was a 125!

The excitement as the holiday brochure dropped on to the mat at home in early January, flicking through to find the camp to go on for that summer was all part of the experience of camps and house parties. And as the years went on, the overseas CRUSOE expeditions appeared, other camps became available, groups had their own camps and residential opportunities. But all through it was the ideal opportunity of having a personal encounter with the Lord Jesus, being away from the peer pressure at home, the family situation at home and many young people have come to faith because of the role of the camp, house party or other residential opportunity offered to them as youngsters.

*   *   *

Crusader Camp Calls

Ian Wherry, Watford Crusaders

"Oooorderleeees" The drawn out call echoed across the field covered in rows of bell tents and a few larger rectangular ones. That meant that a meal would soon be ready, as it was a call for the "duty" tents to their table duties. It was one of many calls that regulated the routine of a Crusader Camp, in the third quarter of the 20th century.

At the beginning of the day, a bell stirred the campsite to life; soon followed by the first shout of the day, "biscuits", an encouragement to get out of one's sleeping bag and being served at a location close to the ablution trestle tables, encouraged a wash. Calm returned as "Quiet Time" was called and each tent officer shared some Christian teaching and prayer, having been guided by one of the padres as to the format.

"Officers" was the next call when the tent officers and camp executive met to pray over the day's activities. Meanwhile the tent occupants were hopefully preparing for the next call: "Tent Inspection", taken very seriously by most as there was a prize for the best. The first "Orderly" call then preceded the breakfast bell. Would the porridge today be of wallpaper paste consistency or building blocks?

After breakfast was morning prayers and before the activities of the day, came the call "Canteen Opening"; Then there was the choice of possibly podex, crocker, medicine ball, halo, table tennis, chess and a variety of special events such as "Camp Fair" and "Hunt The Officer" featured on particular days. For the less energetic, there was the possibility of exploring the rock pools, or a trip to the local town. Later the eagerly awaited "Bathing Party" call sounded. We had to be sure we had our "buddy" to keep an eye on us and vice versa. One day featured a day trip to places of interest in the area, what would the packed lunch contain?

After dinner, the call came for "Siesta", half an hour confined to ones tent, a good time to get that postcard written. Activities and calls repeated themselves until tea was over, when the chant went up: "Please Mr Rag Man may we have the Rag please?" A not too accurate but often highly entertaining account of camp activities and personalities followed. Evening events usually centred around various games except on Sunday when there was a Bible Scavenger Hunt or when there was a Rag Concert where many budding thespians or comedians made a start. The evening call for "Officers" heralded the last phase of the day, the call for "Evening Prayers" following, when CSSM choruses would reverberate around the field to guitar accompaniments. On conclusion cocoa and a bun would be served before we were ushered into our tents for "Quiet Time", an opportunity to expand and discuss the evening's subject. All too soon came the final call: "Lights Out" and for another day a hush descended over the campsite... well sort of!

West Herts Crusader Camp, St. Davids, Wales, August 1966

West Herts Crusader Camp, Treyarnon Bay, Cornwall, August 1963

West Herts Crusader Camp, St Davids, Wales 1967

West Herts Crusader Camp, Treyarnon Bay, Cornwall in the 1960s

I Could Be Myself

Robert Graham, Buckhurst Hill Crusaders

A younger lad in my cub pack invited me to my local Crusaders class in Buckhurst Hill, Essex in 1970. I was ten years old and in my final year at primary school. Buckhurst Hill was a large class, one of the biggest in the area, as I soon learnt from hearing the "returns" which were read out weekly. Indeed the class grew steadily in the 1970s and each time an attendance record was broken so was an old 78rpm record broken over our leader Ray Allison's head!

Due to the dedication of many leaders at Buckhurst Hill we enjoyed many activities, football in the winter and those classic Crusader games Crocker and podex in the summer. There were also class holidays on the canals at Easter and a Whit Camp each year on the banks of the River Thames at Little Stoke near Goring in Oxfordshire. We were also encouraged to go on the Crusader Union holidays.

The atmosphere at both the local class and national camps was caring and encouraging. Although not at all musical, I found the choruses we sang from *Youth Praise* book very moving and through an economy of words the

Christian truths were taken to heart and remembered. Choruses such as "Living he loved me, dying he saved me also In my need Jesus found me".

I became a Christian at a Crusader New Years House Party at Nash Court 1973/74. The many friendships made at camps were maintained by letter writing. At that time while doing a Red Bus rover around London with a school friend I visited Crusader HQ at Ludgate Hill, there Jack Watford took time to have an encouraging word with us. Crusaders was a welcome contrast from the highly academic independent school I attended where you were only called by your surname and residential activities generally centred on the combined cadet force.

A generation later it has been my privilege to be on the staff when both my son and daughter attended their first Crusader holiday at Sandle Manor and Pinewood respectively. They have both continued to attend Crusader holidays. Driving back from Portsmouth Harbour after picking my daughter up from her Westbrook holiday this summer I asked her why she had enjoyed it so much, she replied, "I could be myself, the leaders were so friendly and I could ask the questions I really wanted to ask" an answer I could have given thirty years earlier. Although post holiday contact and fellowship is now maintained by MSN and texting the Christian message and essence and warmth of Crusaders is as essential now as it ever was.

*   *   *

Lone Crusaders

Rosemary Landreth, Brentwood Crusaders

At a time when more children than today were sent to boarding school, a scheme called 'Lone Crusaders' was set up in which the young person at school was linked with an adult leader who corresponded with him/her and sent a regular Bible study which was then sent back to the leader for correction and comment. I was involved with this for several years and have a particularly vivid memory of the study I did in the book of Esther. At my 70th birthday party one of my former school friends told us that my regular Bible studies had made a great impression on her at this time.

In 1942 at the age of 12, I attended a League of Pioneers holiday. These were an important part of the Christian young people's scene in Britain, and at this holiday I met people who were also Crusaders. When I went to Oxford in 1948 I found a number of fellow Crusaders in the CU, not least one who is still one of my dearest friends and another, Gordon Landreth, who has been my husband for 53 years and was himself converted through membership of the Welwyn Garden City class. I became involved as a 'Junior Officer' at several house parties during my student days and was a helper at the Putney class while doing my teacher training in London.

When my husband and I returned to the UK after 14 years in the Colonial Service in Nyasaland (Malawi) we settled in Brentwood where we immediately found fellow Crusaders and from 1969-1981 I was a co-leader of the class with Jenny Barfoot and Joan Dewhirst. During this period I was also a member of the Council for a short time. So, my lonely studies as a young teenager continued to influence my life many years later.

My family's connections with Crusaders have continued and our 2 daughters, one son-in-law and grandchildren all owe a huge debt to the organisation. Our older daughter, Jenny was involved in several holidays and met her husband, Chris Carrington, at the Clarens Holiday in Switzerland in 1972. Chris became a Christian through his membership of the Solihull class and was a leader there for 25 years as well as helping at several house parties and camps. Our younger daughter, Sue Bruce, was a member of the Brentwood class from 1969 – 1980, attended several house parties both as a member and as a helper, and was a member of the Youth Council for a while. She also worked with Careforce for a year as a result of Crusader connections.

The influence of Crusaders continues into the next generation. Our eldest grandchildren, Ruth and Peter Carrington, were both members of Solihull Class (as is younger sister Helen) for many years and have been going to Crusader holidays every year since they were 9 years old – as helpers and assistant leaders for the past few years. They would both look back to these holidays as the main points of spiritual growth in their lives. Studland for Ruth and Westbrook for Peter are very much their spiritual homes.

*   *   *

A Welshman By Birth!

Klaus Marx, Putney Crusaders

In the days before Union camping became the norm, Putney Crusaders held two house-parties of a fortnight each at Llanfairfechan on the North Wales coast. I had been attending Crusaders since the end of 1943, invited by a fellow pupil at my school, who dropped out a few weeks later and left me in the class. Such are God's extraordinary ways!

In August 1947 I was attending the class house-party as I had done in the previous three years. One night, being very much one of the lads, I inaugurated a raid, well armed with pillows on an adjacent dormitory. Battle had been fully joined when up the stairs came our class leader, the formidable E P Olney, known to everyone by his nickname 'Aunt'. He hauled me out on to the landing and pronounced that I would sleep there for the duration of the night. As I lay there sleepless on the hard floorboards, I had ample time to reflect upon my self-centred way of life, and the pointlessness of it, and the need to reform.

That was the beginning of a momentous week. Because all the Sunday evening services in the village were in Welsh, it was a tradition to climb up the lower slopes of Penmaenmawr mountain for what came to be dubbed 'The sermon on the Mount'. The talk that evening was on Mark 8 v34 'If anyone would come after Me, he must deny himself and take up his cross and follow Me.' There and then, amidst the endless swatting of midges in the evening gloaming, I surrendered my life to the Lord Jesus, and have never looked back.

Many years later at a service at a chapel at Menai Straits I was asked to share my testimony. I was able to create an instant rapport with the congregation by announcing that, despite my strange sounding name, I was a Welshman by birth!

Castlerock, Guysmere. Crusaders!

Henry Armstrong, Londonderry Crusaders

Just to hear any of these words mentioned reminds me of my first experience of a Crusader Camp. It was held in the grounds of Guysmere, a large house in Castlerock a small town in County Londonderry, Northern Ireland. Guysmere was the perfect setting for a camping holiday, being situated on a raised green on the edge of the beach on which the Atlantic breakers rolled in. My brother had been a member of the Londonderry Crusader Class about five years before I joined and had become a Christian at a house party at St Valerie's County Dublin.

I attended the Londonderry Class from 1947 — 1952 each Sunday afternoon and also Crusader Camps and house-parties, the latter were held in accommodation at Strickland's Glen, Bangor, County Down. My memories of my first Camp include the panic I felt when the train arrived at Castlerock and we made our way to Guysmere, the hard uneven ground on which I tried to sleep and keep warm in a makeshift sleeping bag, the midnight feast(s)! The Spartan bathes at 7.30 a.m., being last to be allocated a team when sides were picked for games! Yes, I do remember these very well, but above all I remember coming to faith, following a challenging talk, during the singing of the hymn "How sweet the name of Jesus sounds in a believer's ear…" The date was August 14th 1948.

My life since that momentous decision has been a bit of a roller-coaster – there have been times of great blessing and enthusiasm but there have also been periods of great struggles – however through thick and thin I have kept "Looking unto Jesus".

The weekly meetings held in the little back room, up a rather rickety staircase of the Presbyterian Working Men's

Institute, where we heard a thoughtful talk and learned wonderful hymns and choruses, have had a profound influence on my life.

In 1972 I obtained a post in Southport. I knew no-one in Southport so I asked T.S. Mooney my former Crusader Leader, with whom I had kept in touch, if there were Crusaders in that town. T.S., as he was affectionately known, wrote to a Crusader leader in the area, C.D.M. Roberts J.P. "I'm sure the old boy will help you" or words to that effect. The "Old Boy" turned out to be a young dentist in his early thirties who held a Crusader Class in his home. David Roberts and his wife extended tremendous hospitality to me until my wife and family joined me. Thirty-four years later David still passes on to me all the Crusader news and now includes 'Engage'.

I have found a total commitment of life to God, deep Biblical knowledge and integrity of life in all the Crusader Leaders whom I have had the privilege and joy to meet at Camps, House-parties and in other spheres of life. The emphasis has always been on God's Word and the gospel has been preached simply, directly and effectively, T.S.Mooney's aim was, in his own words, "to give every boy a Book in his hand, a Saviour in his heart and a purpose in his life". I can think of no better advice from a Crusader Leader.

*   *   *

Campsite Memories

Colin D. Forbes, Birkenhead Crusaders

I was a member of Birkenhead Crusaders from 1943; the leaders were Will Rankin, Sidney Proctor (great Cru camper) and George Wainwright. I received my Crusader Knighthood Bible in November 1944, (much noted and marked therein over the years from SU notes and Scripture Gift Mission Certificates.) Class numbers reached 100+. There were great birthday celebrations with Cecil J Allen, the Cru Committee member and renowned Railway expert showing his films of legendary steam trains, and also a talk from Cru President on Prov. 3 vv 5-6: if these words worked for him through his life, then they too set me up for my journey of faith and discipleship to a personal Saviour and a most providential marriage.

I enjoyed numerous camps, and the fellowships therein, details of which are shown below:

First – *1946 Studland:* No swims since many wartime coastal anti invasion defences were still in place. We had to help on the farm too. Great field of weeds uphill from the camp site. 'There be rows of Kale planted in there' and so there were, all cleared for the farmer by the end of camp, between rows of hand pulled weeds by scarred and scratched Crusaders.

Second – *1948 Red Wharf Bay on Anglesey:* Climbed up Snowdon and much Welsh spoken.

Third – *1949 St David's Head, SW Wales:* Elevated to Tent Officer of wonderful 8 person bell tent. Two rows of them with marquee at each end for meetings and grub. Wonderful site not far from the Cathedral of St David and the sea for swims among the seals. Stayed behind after Thursday departures as rear-guard to drop, fold and pack tents etc. Drew short straw to clean and dismantle the holes in the ground Loos! With public transport dominant in those days, the Cru Camps ran from Tuesdays to Thursdays to avoid heavy weekend holiday travel.

Fourth & Fifth *1952 & 1953* – Wonderful Polzeath on north Cornish coast.

Sixth – *1954 Westbrook II:* Elevated to STADJY, i.e. Assistant Adjutant. Dwelt in thatched open hut by the two rows of tents by the Hacker court!

God bless Crusaders, and what a foundation for Urban Saints to build on and adapt to changing society since the Kingdom of God as declared by Christ as the Son of Man is the same yesterday, today and forever!

*   *   *

A Horizon Broadened

Peter Meldrum, Birkenhead School Crusaders

In the late nineteen-fifties school boys, such as myself, at a Cheshire school, had a narrow horizon. A Crusader camp holiday broadened my horizon and provided my first holiday away from home with boys of my own age. Birkenhead School, in Cheshire, had a large and flourishing Crusader group. As evangelicals we did not meet in the school's large Anglican chapel on Sundays but in a cellar classroom. My school attendance thus extended to seven days a week.

The summer Crusader camp at Polzeath in Cornwall attracted half a dozen boys from our school group and we travelled together under the supervision of a group leader. The journey itself was an adventure in those days involving a late night departure from Liverpool by steam train. Throughout the night we puffed and shunted and didn't arrive in Cornwall until midday the next day. It was quite a sight to see two huge steam locomotives coupled together pulling our train up the long Devon hills.

Of the camp, I can remember that organisation was along military lines with an Adjutant and other officers in charge. Accommodation was in bell tents. Worship and meals took place in large marquees. The last activity of the day was a quiet time in tents with our Bibles. All round it was a wonderful holiday: the beautiful beach was nearby, and I recall seeing, for the first time, a sea with surfable waves. With the strong Bible based Crusader spirit, fellowship flourished. We boys found that there were Crusader groups and a world outside Cheshire.

*   *   *

A Lifelong Mission Started at Camp

Rev Roger Campbell, Nottingham Crusaders

 My brother and I joined the Nottingham Crusader Class in 1952. We were taken along by someone from school and found that we knew quite a few of the other boys.

The following Easter we went to a house party at a school in Market Harborough. The Commandant was a Mr Ken Thornberry, who worked for the Africa Inland Mission. It was during that weekend that I invited Christ into my life. I sensed that a significant change had taken place in my relationship with Jesus though I couldn't have explained it at the time. As we were leaving the weekend, Mr Thornberry gave me a few back copies of the AIM magazine. That began a twenty year connection with the mission, and a lifelong interest in mission work.

Each year we went to a Crusader Camp in the summer. The first one was at Sidestrand on the East Coast in 1953, followed by St. David's in 1954 and Stoke Fleming in 1955. I really enjoyed these camps and the Christian input gave me a boost to keep me going. Of course we had the regular Sunday afternoon classes, but the camps were special.

I kept up the connection with Crusaders until I went to University. By that time I had discovered the existence of Evangelical Anglican churches, and so got involved with Pathfinder camps.

I have always been grateful to God for the teaching and help that Crusaders gave me as a young teenager, setting me on the road of discipleship. Some years later, I became an Anglican minister, and then worked with CMS in Singapore. But it all began with Crusaders!

What has God in store for me?

Roxana Peters, Smallwood Camps

My first Crusader holiday was in 1999. I had met Daphne Dew at a weekend training session, where I was doing the food and hygiene course or was it the first aid? It certainly wasn't in preparation for a Crusader camp! Other courses were being run, so there were plenty of people there. As most of those attending were young (i.e. under 35) and I was somewhat older, I gravitated to the kitchen in any spare time and gave Daphne a hand with the washing up. Daphne catered for all Crusader HQ events as well as at least one holiday a year at that time. By the end of the weekend she had convinced me she needed someone to help at a children's holiday that summer – I can wash up, so agreed. A few weeks later I was flattered when Daphne asked me to assist her plan the menu and shopping lists.

As the Camp approached, we went shopping and planned the journey. It was all new, exciting and unknown. Daphne was a wonderful companion and explained things so well that I felt at home at Smallwood from early on. I still harboured the notion that I would be washing up, but Daphne had other ideas and her confidence in me was a revelation. She was training me up as assistant caterer, with a view to caterer! Although I have enjoyed cooking all my adult life I have never aspired to cook for 60, 70 or 80 people.

We spent the first hours alone in the beautiful building, preparing for the team's arrival. Keith and Celia arrived and so did the team they had drawn together who in a short while would defy expectations and become a unit with a single purpose; to open the eyes of the children to the unfailing love of Jesus.

I remember laughs, fun, tiredness, satisfaction and a strong sense of the Lord in all the activities during the week. Alton Towers was the big attraction for the children, but Daphne put her encyclopaedic knowledge of the area to good use and arranged a 'Cooks' Tour'. After seeing the children and leaders off to Alton Towers and making sure the evening meal would be ready for their return, we set off. A bit of sightseeing, a beautiful place for lunch, time to relax and get to know each other, a cream tea somewhere and then back, refreshed. At the end of the week came the banquet! Oh the fun of putting that and the evening concert together and then packing up to go home the next day. One of the most demanding, self-imposed challenges of the camp!

And that was the first of several camps run on the same lines with different leaders and teams. And they were all special; we rarely had the same team in the kitchen, and God overruled our differences and made each one work well; meals were on time and (usually) well received. Regrettably camp was cancelled in 2011 and as I write I have a deep sadness but so many memories; of children coping with being away from home, the sense of family encouraged by Keith and Celia's example, evening services, wide games, fire practices, water games, and children coming to faith even as the faith of us leaders was deepened.

What a very special privilege. Thank you Crusaders – for such you were when I started – for the opportunity to serve my Lord in this way.

Unforgettable Camps

Jeremy Nutter, Leigh on Sea Crusaders

Commy, Adjy, Stadjy, Puddox, Crocker, Halo and The Lord – My Saviour were all familiar words to a Crusader in the 60s and 70s. As a seven year old, church, for me was dull; it was dark, the pews were hard, you couldn't talk, you didn't understand what was going on and it happened once a week. Crusaders and Mini Crus to which I was introduced by my best friend Andrew, were entirely different. Ten Sundays of attendance and you got your badge; fifty Sundays and you got your badge embossed Bible, which I still proudly own.

Sunday meetings were uplifting, engaging and provided you with the freedom to make your own decisions. There were competitions with exciting Christian book prizes, Sword drill which taught you the books of the Bible, lively uplifting choruses one of which ended 'Well done my brave Crusader' and break-out groups to discuss the application of Christianity.

During the winter there were house groups for hobbies and fellowship. In the summer we met in a field and played Crusader games and prayed! For a young lad this was what I needed and so the foundations of my faith today were laid at Crusaders.

But there was more. There were the wonderful summer camps at Westbrook, Studland, St David's and also the unforgettable Isles of Scilly. It was at these that I learnt many of my life skills. How to get on with complete strangers and make friends, how to have fun whilst away from home, self-discipline, personal hygiene, working as a team, helping others. This was Christianity in action. The morning and evening Bible studies in our tents were a joy, often lit by Tilley lamps they were small and intimate, with some of us balancing precariously on over filled palliasses and others feeling uncomfortable with their under filled palliasses.

But it didn't matter, as the love of Christ surrounded each and every one of us. And then there were the evening meetings led by Padre. We all wanted to go, Christian and non-Christian alike, no dissenters. We sang familiar and less familiar songs to guitar music. The talk was illustrated, relevant and spoke to each of us in different ways and of course we learnt of the following day's activities.

Amongst my more bizarre memories I can remember two lads being cut off by the tide at the Old Harry Rocks in Studland. I remember climbing the Agglestone rock, reputedly a missile launched by the Devil from the Isle of White at Corfe castle. I remember six of us in a two man tent riding out a storm on the Isles of Scilly and who could forget the green porridge at Westbrook reputedly as a result of Adjy drying his socks over the pan!

Crusaders was great. It set me up well and it set my father up well some twenty five years earlier.

Well done Crusaders!

* * *

Help On The Hills

Ken Buckler

In 1946, I went to St Bees climbing camp led by Commy John Laing, who arranged for a lorry to carry us each day to the base of a climb somewhere in the Lake District. I was in Tent 1 and the proud possessor of a Baby Box Brownie camera, 3inches cube in size.

On the day we climbed Helvellyn from Glenridding I needed all the handholds I could manage to scramble up Striding Edge. So I pushed my treasured Baby Box Brownie down the front of my pullover. The inevitable happened. As I groped my way up the slippery path my jumper came loose at the waist and my Box Brownie bounced out down 200 feet of rocky cliff towards Red Tarn which lies below the climb. I was heartbroken, but I had been told God answers prayers; so I sent up an SOS prayer. My immediate help came from nimble footed campers who clambered down the precipitous scree avoiding deep crevasses and huge boulders, and found my precious camera sitting on a platform of rock jutting out over Red Tarn. But the lens, less than 2 cms diameter wide, had fallen out.

I remember thinking 'Thank you God but You've not done a very good job – No point in looking for the tiny lens.' We climbed back up to the path, but one of the leaders, Docco Ford, who amongst other things was a keen wild flower collector, found under a flower my camera lens. I learnt two lessons: don't push your camera down the front of your jumper and God loves to answer prayer. I stuck a bit of plaster over a crack in the camera and it worked as well as ever for several years.

God even finds boats and makes provision

One year I went as Padre on the Seamanship Camp based at Botley. It started badly as John Douglas, the leader, had arranged for a number of boats to take us out into the Solent, but a week before the event, one had been returned damaged and unseaworthy. After phoning everyone on the South coast, he managed to hire a replacement.

As we arrived we learnt that another boat had been damaged. John was again phoning everyone who might help – only to be told 'You must be joking. This is high season, and it took a miracle to get the last one', I had to face the troops. What could I say? 'Pray for another miracle' or say 'The Lord wants us to learn to share, which means on the day we don't go out to sea we can have turns in the dinghies on the river'. We felt the former was God's way, so with the boys we prayed for a replacement. The impossible miracle occurred and the RAF Officers' Mess lent us their 'gin palace' which was at least seaworthy in good weather. We all rejoiced together (Incidentally several years later I heard a young leader, not realising that I had been present, tell of this event saying how he learnt then that God does answer prayer).

I travelled with a different boat each day. One day we were stormbound in Weymouth and I was dropped off next morning near Osborne House on the Isle of Wight, to be collected later at Cowes by another boat. I had a pleasant walk to East Cowes and waited on the jetty. It was a lovely sunny day and I was getting hungry and hot but no boat appeared. Early evening I realised I was marooned. To catch the ferry across to Southampton, I had to get a boat across the river and I was penniless. I decided to ring my fiancée, who was staying with her parents at Gosport on the mainland. I found a phone box, contacted the operator and asked to put through a reverse charge call to Gosport.

'Why don't you phone yourself?' she asked. 'Because I haven't any money.' I replied. 'You must have to have got through to me. Press Button B'. I did and out popped two penny pieces.

The long suffering operator then put through my call to Gosport and so I could tell Janet why I'd be late and I arranged to meet her in Southampton at the ferry terminal. I now had two pence to catch the boat across to West Cowes. At the police station I explained my problem and was told they were not allowed to lend money to anyone. One kind officer did lend me a pound to catch the Southampton ferry. I was met by Janet and returned for a late supper to base at Botley, full of gratitude to the Lord and my unrealising angel helpers.

The Moorland Trek

When I was working as an Office Boy at Crusader HQ at Ludgate Hill, (an out of work post-graduate student) there was a need for an Adjutant at Stoke Fleming camp. The camp was in danger of closing as one of the great attractions at Stoke Fleming had been boating on the river Dart estuary, but this was not available. I went down, very ill prepared; no watch or whistle, but full of enthusiasm.

I considered trekking on Dartmoor as a possible new venture. So I arranged to take a party of senior boys on a 'sleep-over'. We left camp pretty exhausted as we'd spent the previous night holding down the main marquee which a gale seemed determined to carry from the camp site over the sea to France. After a bus ride to the edge of Dartmoor we set off exploring the many farmsteads marked on our map. By early evening we found that all the farmsteads we'd located were only piles of ancient stones. We came to the edge of the moor having not met anyone all day.

I was desperate and prayed an SOS 'help' prayer. I left my assistant to keep the boys cheerful and walked down the road where I'd seen a man cutting his hedge. I asked him if he knew of any barn where we might shelter overnight. He laughed, 'This is the height of harvest time – they're all full. But wait a moment, there is one down the road. A townie has bought it and I think I saw him drive in just now.' I ran down and met the townie just driving away. He kindly stopped and I explained our predicament. He understood, handed me the keys of the barn and house and drove off saying 'Just drop the keys through the letter box when you leave.' When I brought the boys to their overnight home, I collapsed on the straw, thanked God and fell fast asleep.

Tales of a Camp Banker / Dining-Room Manager

Ted Talbot

It was a Saturday afternoon in August and the telephone conversation went a little bit like this:

"Ted speaking."

"Oh Hi Ted, Neil Barber here, are you alright?"

"Yes fine thanks Neil"

"That's great Ted – er – where are you?"

"Actually I'm at home, just about to drop into the swimming pool, why?"

"Well, M & M started today and we have a hundred campers wanting to handover their money to the banker!" Dead silence…

"But Neil, M&M starts *next* Saturday"

"No Ted, M&M started today!" Another dead silence…

"Give me 30 minutes and I'll call you back."

Not so much of a problem one might say – except that I live in Switzerland! Well, to cut a long story short I did manage to walk through the door of The Royal Wolverhampton School mid afternoon on Sunday, to much laughter and embarrassment!

M&M of course started its days at Smallwood Manor and accommodation was rather basic and in rather short supply! Dining Room Manager didn't carry much seniority, so one year I slept with a dozen cellos and double-basses. Another year I got thrown out by one of my roommates (Matt remembers) because of my snoring. I didn't tell anyone where I found a secret corner to sleep – but actually it was under a grand piano in one of the meeting rooms.

The Smallwood Cook & Kitchen teams were wonderful and we would dream up exotic ideas for the camp 'banquet night'. One year we decided to hold the banquet on the lawns with the kids being served at table by the officers in DJ's. With over 100 kids on site, finding tables and benches was a challenge. We managed to get the dining room 12 foot oak benches out through the windows ... but where to find tables? After several phone calls a supply was located – at the local old people's home. Into the mini-van we piled and were soon loading tables out the back door of the home much to the consternation of the residents who thought they were being evacuated – or worse! This impression of uncertainty was somewhat heightened by the appearance of at least two Father Christmas' at the windows, who then popped in for a chat! (There were at least 12 Father Christmas' roaming Uttoxeter at that moment being wildly pursued by hordes of campers, so the old people's home was a safe haven!).

One final reminiscence: In the good old days, virtually any adult was authorized to drive the mini-vans – even Dining Room Managers! On one occasion Neil handed me the keys with a muttered "I don't think there's much petrol." Well we arrived at Stafford or wherever it was OK, but on leaving the car park in search of a petrol station in rush hour... yes we ran out! Well it was a quite a tourist attraction to see a mini-van negotiating the main street with 12 kids pushing – and a police escort!

*   *   *

Hunt the Officer

Arthur Cross, Leicester Evington Crusaders

I joined Leicester Evington in 1953 when a friend from school asked if I would like to go along. That was my first contact with Jesus Christ in any meaningful way and led to my own spiritual awakening a few years later.

I went to my first camp as a 17 year old heading off to the Pioneer Camps in Anglesey. I learnt how to fill a 'paillasse' with straw and disguise myself as a Belisha beacon in 'hunt the officer'. I was only discovered by the younger campers because a bee or wasp stung me on my leg as I stood by the roadside!

*   *   *

Nefyn's Football Supporters

Nick Rank, Bramhall Crusaders

Nick Rank told the following story at a prayer meeting recently:

"I was at Nefyn Crusader Camp in 1966 as a 15 year old and we were there on World Cup final day; England v West Germany. A group of us trooped off to Nefyn village and stood on the pavement outside the one electrical shop watching the final on the TV in the window in black and white and with no sound. I guess we made enough noise as England scored four times to be heard across the whole village."

(Nefyn Crusader Camps first ran from 17-25 August 1962 and will be celebrating 50 years in 2012 – Congratulations Nefyn! Ed.)

*   *   *

Fun, Craziness and Laughter At Nefyn

Roger Taylor

I have been on 12 Nefyn camps, all as a leader, each year from 1995 to 2004 inclusive (including two camps back-to-back in 1999), and more recently in 2009. All bar one of these camps has been the 14-16/14-17 year olds camp. For nine of these camps I was tent leader, 1999 saw me, curiously, on the catering team – and on the most recent (2004 and 2009) I was pastoral support and bookshop attendant respectively.

What has Nefyn meant to me? A lot – and not easy to put into print; It has brought me into contact with a lot of wonderful people. (It would be invidious to mention names but Chris Mullan, Dan Mullan, Jo Hill, Sally-Jo Howe, Dave Watkinson – take a bow!) It has enabled me to work for God's kingdom by sharing my faith with and listening to these young people – sometimes very vulnerable (even damaged) youngsters. Nefyns over the years have taught me that young people grow and mature in Christ – I can never forget some of the teenagers' testimonies over the years in the big marquee, for example. I knew, of course, that people grow spiritually, but it is so wonderful to see it, learn from it, be encouraged by it… and build on it.

Apart from all the above the camps have given me unforgettable memories, some really good and deep friendships… and a great deal of fun, craziness and laughter. I think I need only give a passing mention to my now classic "book review" of 1996.

Perhaps unusually, Nefyn has also meant the support and sensitivity shown to me by the young people themselves – for example, when I was tent-leading only a couple of weeks after my mother's death from cancer in 1997. On a happier note, I have been to several weddings of people I have known from Nefyn, notably Howard and Andrea Jones, Rob and Cheryl Cross and Sandy and Liz Cockran.

* * *

A Culinary Delight

Delphine Evans. (Now living in Paris, France)

In 1998 and 2000 I went to the Nefyn camps which will always remain a really special memory for me. Even after all the years that have gone by since the summers I spent there, I can still picture the campsite and the path that led down the hill to Nefyn beach!

I well remember the friendly atmosphere and the enthusiasm and energy of all the people who took part – from the campers to the leaders and their families. Some of the people I met at Nefyn are still close friends today, which bears testament to the special bonds that the camp seems to create.

Each day Nefyn began with a run-down of the planned activities for the day- introduced of course by Howard a.k.a "H" and his famous run and swing around the pole in the main marquee! Amongst the more famous outings were canoeing, abseiling, pottery at Porthmadog and of course, the day trip to Butlins! Every night many different, special ideas and prayers were shared at the evening meetings. I remember the afternoons spent swimming in the sea and, perhaps most famously, 'Spot the Leader' game on the beach with the excellent disguises on display! I will also never forget the culinary delight that was eggy bread, and the song that Roger Taylor sang about it to the tune of '*Oh When the Saints*':

> "*Oh eggy bread*
> *Is wonderful*
> *Oh eggy bread is wonderful*
> *It is eggy, and it is bready*
> *Oh eggy bread is wonderful!*"

*   *   *

The World of Adventure

Rev Joseph Cotterill, Gillingham Crusaders

My first contact with Crusaders was in 1947, not as a boy but as a leader of a class. I had returned from seven years missionary service in North China and Mongolia and I was living in Gillingham, Kent. I was approached by the late Kenneth Anderson, the leader of the class in Rochester, to ask for my help in leading the class. He had to be away often since he was the engineer "digging" the Tyne tunnel. I agreed to help him, until I returned to China. This never happened because of the Communist takeover. Little did I know that I would be leading Crusader classes until 1982! In 1955 I moved to Sidcup and lead there whilst starting classes in Erith and Bexley as well as helping in a class at Eltham College.

Shortly after moving to Sidcup I was invited to serve on the Camps Committee. Later I was asked to serve as Chairman of the Mixed Holidays Committee.

My involvement with Crusader Camps began with Studland in 1948. In 1953 I was asked by the late Maurice Richards to go with him, as Padre, on the first Crusader expedition abroad. 21 of us spent four weeks in Algeria, trekking in a northern spur of the Atlas Mountains, and climbing Mount Tamgout de Lala Khidiga. We went without tents or stoves and depended on finding clean water streams and firewood for each night's camp. The following year we went to the Cevennes in France. Maurice then took parties to the Pyrenees and Norway amongst other places and I was asked for a time to start light weight camps in the UK. The first was on the Isle of Arran, then Western Isles of Scotland, then the Cairngorms in 1957 and Snowdonia in 1958.

In 1959 I returned to leading expeditions abroad, the first one to the Austrian Alps. In 1960 I took a party of 48 boys to Yugoslavia, starting from Sarajevo and walking across the area of Bosnia-Herzegovina to Mostar and Split. 1962 I took a party of 40 boys in 4 vehicles across Europe to follow the footsteps of St. Paul in Greece and then into Italy.

In 1964 a party of 48 of us sailed past the volcano in the sea actively forming the island of Sertsey to Iceland, and trekked in the southern region near Mount Hekla. In 1967 we repeated the trip to Greece, Peloponnese and Italy, this time with a mixed party of boys and girls. The following year we took a mixed party to Sicily, climbing Mount Etna while it was erupting. 1970 saw mixed groups to Oberammergau, Austria and to Iceland. In 1971 we visited the 7 churches of the Revelation in Turkey. In 1972 a party of 24 flew to Toronto, drove in four vehicles to the Canadian Rockies, down into the USA to visit Yellowstone National Park, before returning to Toronto. In 1973 a smaller party visited Israel, this time staying in Youth Hostels and travelling in four hired cars. In the intervening and following years I also helped to lead holidays in this country. I would enjoy hearing from any who took part in these adventures.

After retirement from the Scientific Civil Service in the 1980's, I was ordained into the Church of England and at the age of 94 I am still taking services on a regular basis.

*   *   *

Crusoe (Crusaders Overseas Expeditions)

Heather Hale

So, you're sitting high up, examining the tan lines on your feet... wondering whether it's dirt or tan and then your toes start getting painted... squinting through the harsh sunlight rippling through the slatted windows, a cheeky face smiles back at you. The man walks down the carriage all through the night with cries of 'Chai-Coppy', but I don't mind. The tea is so sweet that it's like half the cup is full of sugar. You can't have it any other way. Running through my mind are the children. Their joy and our return to the college, the way they run and follow us wherever we are, curious as to who these strange people are painting their nursery and climbing frame. They love the balloons and the parachute and the train set. Our face paints and wool are in constant use. Ultimately, however we're here to tell these children about Jesus, through our sketches and games. That truly is the best gift we can give them.

This is a familiar story of a young person taken out of their comfort zone and exposed to the other half of the world. The sights and smells, memories and friends stay with you for life. Mine was India in about 1997 and Crusaders has been challenging young people for years through Crusoe

and will continue to in the future. Such is the success of Crusoe, touching lives and changing individuals for ever. I'm one of those people. Crusoe taught me to challenge and know the difference between the words "need" and "want".

Two little words with totally different meanings; relying on God is easy when life's straightforward, you go to school, your parents provide for you and everything's easy... stepping out of that comfort zone, you really understand what trusting in God is about and that is something you can then build your life upon. I've taken my Crusaders experiences and used them as lessons. I've enjoyed leading several Crusoe trips since, supporting teams going on Crusoe and team members, leading Crusader groups and helping at other Crusader events.

Crusaders and particularly working with other volunteers within Crusaders has taught me what it means to give of yourself – whole-heartedly, unconditionally and selflessly, to others and particularly to young people. The late nights, the worn out look on your face and being shattered for a week afterwards, but doing it laughing and smiling, with a joke or a song, with happiness in your heart – this is what I've learnt through Crusaders that this is giving as God calls us to.

*   *   *

Seven and a Half Weeks in Peru

Ali Tompkins

It was a very different 21st birthday that I celebrated in 1988 sitting outside a Bible School building project in Accobamba, on the outskirts of Tarma in Peru. My parents had sent out a small birthday present which included a book – 'Paddington Bear at the Laundrette'! Over lunch, Douglas Edmonds took great delight in reading the book to us.

My friend Carrie and I had decided in November the previous year that we wanted to do something different in the summer. I had spent most of my summers on Crusader holidays, first as a girl then as a leader. We applied and attended the selection weekend in the February and by the middle of July we were off to the other side of the world.

The Peruvian Christians made us so welcome. We spent 5 weeks working with them and amongst them on the building project that had been started the year before through EUSA (now Latin Link). I came home a qualified 'Peruvian Bricky' able to dig foundations, mix cement by hand, lay floorboards and carry 'aqua' containers on my shoulder up ladders with the best of them!

The Peruvians are a very 'manana' type people and I remember that one day we had got to the stage in the build that meant if cement didn't arrive the next day, we would have to stop for a few days! Somewhere around 4 or 5 in the morning there was a loud clattering and yelling at the gate across the compound – '*Cemento, cemento*' just in time for the next phase of the build!

Each week we had a day off the build which meant that we could head out somewhere as a team. Bearing in mind that the 'Sendero' were still operating only 2 hours away from where we were the local Missionary was very cautious in advising the best places and would accompany us. We travelled in the back of pick-ups on several occasions, we experienced the delicacies of guinea-pig, we used squat loos and Ann (a team leader) experienced the cold showers daily! (The rest of us spent the weeks unclean, until the local SU missionary family returned and we could use their hot shower!)

We attended the local village church every Sunday and gradually followed the Bible passages, joining in hymns (in English) and learning some Spanish songs. We were invited to a wedding in Tarma, and welcomed by the entire village at the very beginning of our stay having to parade through the street as part of their Celebration Day.

The five weeks disappeared very quickly and with very sad goodbyes we returned to Lima before heading down Cusco. It was so hard having been a part of the community to being a tourist as we visited Macchu Picchu.

The experiences have stayed with me since that year, my passion for South America has never dwindled and it has been a great pleasure to head out to Mexico on the Urban Saints *ReBuild* programme.

*   *   *

Dyffryn 1969

Westbrook 1960

Crusader Associates

Were you a Crusader?

Did you go on a Crusader holiday?

Was much of your Christian teaching and discipleship learnt at Crusaders?

To whom are you passing it on?

'And the things you have heard me say in the presence of many witnesses entrust to reliable men who will also be qualified to teach others.' 2 Timothy 2:2

Become a Crusader Associate and pass on the baton to the next generation

For over one hundred years children and young people have met the Lord through Crusaders, and have gone on to be taught and discipled by faithful men and women of God. We owe so much to those dedicated leaders of the past, many of whom gave their whole lives in service to the movement.

The ministry is still going strong today – the name may be different but the desire to reach young people for Christ remains as passionate as ever.

But what of the future?

'After that whole generation had been gathered to their fathers, another generation grew up, who knew neither the Lord nor what he had done for Israel.' Judges 2:10

The Apostle Paul urges us in 2 Timothy to pass on to others what has been faithfully entrusted to us.

Will you consider becoming a Crusader Associate and ensuring young people still have opportunities to meet Jesus, and be discipled and mentored through Urban Saints?

We need people like you who will pass on the baton to the next generation.

For an annual subscription of £25 we will send you *Crusader Associate News* twice a year. This magazine gives details of what is happening in Urban Saints today with a special emphasis on celebrations of anniversaries and reunions, stories of people you may remember, and news of special interest to those with a history of Crusaders, as well as the 'With Christ' pages. You will also receive invitations to any appropriate national or local events, and the daily prayer diary *Pray4Change*, if requested.

"I've been a Crusader since I was eleven. I haven't run a group for many years but I know it is so important to keep investing in the younger generation. When us old men dream dreams, I want to do all I can to help today's young men in leadership be blessed with the envisioning of the Lord. By being a Crusader Associate, I know I am passing on the baton of what I gained to the next generation."

Allan Plumpton

What Do Urban Saints Do?

The dream of Urban Saints is to release a radical movement of young people, committed to taking the good news of Jesus Christ to every generation.

Our passion is to help young people live lives of faith, hope and love through Jesus Christ.

We do this in two ways:

- by equipping local churches and youth groups with training, resources, support and encouragement. www.urbansaints.org/energize

- by offering life-changing experiences to young people such as events, holidays, community projects and training programmes.

To find out more about becoming a Crusader Associate email: email@urbansaints.org or phone 01582 589850.